Sandspurs and Sawgrass:

A Collection of True Stories from North Florida

For Lisa —
best wishes!
Betsy

Sandspurs and Sawgrass:

A Collection of True Stories from North Florida

By

Betsy James

ISBN: 1-58721-041-X

1stBooks - rev. 11/06/00

About the Book

Sandspurs and Sawgrass – a collection of true stories from North Florida is a work still in progress. North Florida is a unique and largely unspoiled area that is rich in folklore. This book seeks to preserve the stories that abound, for all generations to enjoy.

It is about ghosts, humorous situations, and tales that touch the heart. It is about moonshining, fishing, sinkholes, and dirt-surfing. This is the first edition—there is more to come!

Town

The house had been painted blue a long, long time ago. I was surprised at the starkness of the interior. There were no knick-knacks, and the furniture was sparse. The only wall decoration was a 1949 calendar with a picture of Jesus on it, outstretched hands and a haloed head. An iron frame bed stood along one wall, covered with a faded, well patched quilt. A homemade table filled part of the room, surrounded by mismatched chairs. A very bony woman sat in one of these chairs, eating cookies and looking at me with blank eyes. An equally bony man peered out at me from the kitchen. I could see he was washing dishes.

The journey that had brought me to their doorstep had been filled with minor accidents and bad directions. I had gotten off the interstate to change a flat tire and had taken a wrong turn somewhere. Stopped at a farmhouse to ask directions back to the interstate and ended up lost on dirt roads. Hadn't seen a house for at least ten miles until I spotted this one. The door was open and I now stood in the doorway, wondering where my voice had gone.

"Here," said the woman, holding out her half-eaten package of cookies. I took the cookies and carried them into the kitchen. The man had stopped washing dishes and was staring at me intently. "This is what I do best," he stated. He held up a washcloth which was steadily dripping onto the cracked linoleum. I set the cookies down on the counter and asked if he could direct me back to the Interstate. Or into town - any town where I could buy gas and a road map.

"Could you give Rosie a lift?" he asked.

"Sure," I replied. Just get me into town and I'll take her wherever she needs to go."

He led me onto a back porch, where a short, plump woman was sleeping heavily on the bare boards.

"Rosie," he yelled, "wake up! Your ride's here!" She groggily came to and eyed me suspiciously. She sat up and yawned and for a moment I was afraid she would go back to sleep.

"Jest a minute," she said. "I got to go find Lester." She heaved her bulky form up and disappeared around the corner of the house.

"She'll be right back. She's going to find Lester," explained the man. I followed him back inside to wait for Rosie and whoever Lester was.

"Mama likes her cookies,." he murmured as he took the half-eaten package back in to the bony woman. She began to devour them with a passion I found inconsistent with her skeletal body.

I wondered right then if I was ever going to find civilization again. It seemed like I was going to be stuck out here on dirt roads and in remote farmhouses for the rest of eternity. I didn't even know if I was in Florida or Georgia. The dirt roads were a pale peach color, a mixture of sand and clay. I didn't see a telephone anywhere, or a newspaper or magazine, or anything that might indicate where in the heck I was.

"Set down," invited the woman. "Rosie'll be right back. She went to get Lester," she continued. "Who's Lester?" I asked. "Her goat. She don't go nowhere without Lester," she replied. "I'm driving a Toyota...not much room in the back seat," I suggested.

When Rosie appeared, she was leading a young goat on a dog's leash. It was puppy-size, not the full grown animal I had imagined. "Don't worry. He jest done his business. He won't mess up in your car none," she assured me. I felt thankful for that as she guided him into the back seat of my car, where he immediately began pawing at the windows trying to get out. Rosie got in and we took off down the dirt road, dry dust blowing around us like a low-flying cloud. She told me which turns to take, where to slow down, but she did not offer any converstaion. I made a feeble attempt, remarking on the weather and the fact that we'd had no rain lately, but she didn't reply.

Finally we pulled up at a little country store. It was flanked on both sides by empty buildings and several nearby houses. A sign on the door announced that a U.S. Post Office was located somewhere inside. I filled up my tank, which was running

2

dangerously low, but did not find a road map. Guessed I'd have to leave it up to Rosie to get me into town.

When Rosie emerged, she was carrying a package of cookies and three quarts of Old English 800. "You mind?" she asked as she opened one. "Why should I mind?" I answered, used to the unexpected by now. Or so I thought. Several miles and about a half hour later, I realized that Rosie had fallen asleep again. So I woke her up. "Oops. You done missed the turn," she stated.

"You mean I've been going the wrong way?" I asked in exasperation. "You kin turn around right up here. See that road?" yawned Rosie as she opened up another quart. A few thousand acres of cornfields and woods later, I realized we were approaching the old blue farmhouse. The one where I'd acquired my current passengers. Angrily I pulled up to the house and shut off the car. "I thought you were going to get me into town," I hissed.

"That WAS town," she stated as she coaxed Lester out of the back seat.

The Commissary

Every Fall, his Papa would drive the Model T down to Hosford, from their farm in Sawdust. His Papa would always make the trip first, in order to take care of the business end of the coming venture. He knew that in a few days, he'd be loading sweet potatoes, cane syrup and smoked bacon onto the wagon. It was a fourteen mile trip over a two-rut road through scrub oak forests, to the commissary in Hosford, where the sawmill was.

Early in the morning they'd start out. Him, Charlie Green (the hired helper), Driver (the hound dog) and Belle and Dixie (the two mules who pulled the wagon.) In order to get there, they had to cross three streams. Indian Creek was the first one. It was only ankle deep, so the mules didn't mind fording it one bit. They'd stop for a minute to get 'em a cool drink of water, then move on. Around about this time, him and Charlie Green would get to thinking about the possibility of ice cream. Sometimes it would come into the commissary, packed in ice, from down the river, in Apalachicola. For some reason, it was always vanilla.

Then, they'd come to the second stream, called the Oklawaha. Again, the mules would be no problem fording this shallow creek. Sometimes in the distance they'd hear the donkey trains, moving lumber. These were logging trains. Temporary tracks would be laid throughout the forest. They'd cut all the trees around the train, load it on, then just move the tracks!

Driver would trot alongside the wagon the whole way there, except for chasing an occasional rabbit or squirrel. All would be fine till they reached the third stream, called Hosford Mill Creek. This one had a bridge with no railing, and Belle and Dixie did not like crossing it one bit! They could figure on spending a good bit of time there - pushing, pulling, and bribing those mules. Finally, when they were about ready to give up, Belle and Dixie would decide to cooperate. Of course, him and Charlie Green'd be totally exhausted by this time. They'd begin to think about that tall bottle of Nehi soda waiting for them at the commissary.

When they got there, they'd unload the wagon and refill it with barrels of rice and flour. They'd also get coffee, sugar, canned salmon and salt mullet. Then, they'd start back up that two-rut road for Sawdust, wishing the first bridge had a railing on it!

Author's Footnote: This two-rut road is now Highway 65.

Riding The Crow

Lake Sampala reflected swiftly changing blues and greys of a late afternoon thunderstorm. Cypress trees swayed gracefully in the mounting winds. Waterbirds reluctantly left plentiful waters for the shelter of the forest. It was disturbingly still.

Tommy Tatum dozed contentedly under a stunted pine, his fishing pole propped against an old tire. In his dreams, he drove a tractor over freshly plowed fields, making patterns in the raw dirt. A large black crow followed him, cawing urgently. He looked up and cursed the noisy creature. Suddenly the crow disappeared and he heard an ominous roar. The tractor must be overheating, he reasoned, and reached down and turned off the key. The dream changed, and he was carried off upon the back of the crow, which was considerably larger than he had at first thought it to be. First, his hat blew off and his stump of a cigar flew out of his mouth. The crow began to fly faster and faster, and Tommy hung on for dear life. All of a sudden they landed in the thick bushes and he woke up.

He was scratched and aching all over. And surely not where he was when he went to sleep! As he raised up, he saw trees down and a big path cleared right up to where he was sitting. He remembered throwing a line out into the lake and settling back. How he got to where he was, was a mystery. One thing for sure, though... he needed to get out of the briars and into a safe place. He saw a clearing a little ways off, so he staggered up and made his way through the brambles. When he got to the clearing, he found that it was a road.

Eventually, the storm began to let up and the sounds of thunder to fade. He found it increasingly painful to walk, and began to wonder if he could make it back to civilization. As he hobbled along, though, things began to look more and more familiar. He realized that this was the road he drove in on. And surely enough, a little ways ahead, he saw his truck. As he looked around, it dawned on him what must have happened. Trees that weren't broken off completely were twisted at odd angles. Lake Sampala was covered with debris, and the tree he

7

had fallen asleep under was not there at all! A tornado had come through and picked him up, still sleeping, and set him down in the blackberry bushes!

He was able to drive back to town, but by the time he got there his ankle was beginning to swell, and his bruises and scratches to throb unmercifully. His kinfolk rushed him to the hospital, where he was found to have a fractured ankle. By the next day, he was almost completely purple from head to toe. As the nurses gathered around, all agreeing that it was a miracle he survived, the doctor came in.

"Your guardian angel must have some along right when that tornado did, Tommy Tatum!" the doctor exclaimed.

"Nope," Tommy replied. "Just a big black crow!"

The Drew Mansion

Way back in the late 1800s, Governor George F. Drew built a mansion down by the Suwannee River. It was surrounded by formal gardens, several out-buildings, and magnificent live oaks. Around back there was an old jail. It was a square structure built of stone, rising to about fifteen feet. There was no roof over this jail. Prisoners had to suffer the elements, subsisting on bread and water. Few survived that open pit jail, and it was said the only way out was through the Pearly Gates.

Running in front of the mansion was a railroad track. Governor Drew would catch the train every morning to go to work in Tallahassee. After he finished his term as governor, he moved to Jacksonville. Two other families, the Buckis and then the Millinors lived there. One year there was a terrible flood. That Suwannee River just kept on rising until it crept into the mansion. Children who lived there at that time remember having to move out in the middle of the night. Water was standing six feet deep downstairs! Rowboats were loaded with people and furniture.

The mansion stood abandoned for years. Parquet flooring, antiques, tilework and fixtures were removed, and the old mansion decayed. A sharecropper family moved in for a short time, but moved out rather hurriedly as they were beset by ghosts. Chains heard rattling in the night were attributed to the unfortunate prisoners that were once held out back.

During the early sixties, when the place was grown up so bad you could hardly get in, four young friends decided to make their fortune in the old basement. They got a big kettle, some tubing, and set up a still. This operation proved fruitful for a number of years. One night there was a horrible train wreck just a few hundred feet from the mansion. The tracks had not been kept up for some time, causing the engine and most of the cars to derail.

Afterwards, when the work crew was picking up the last of the wreckage, a familiar odor began to waft past them on the midnight breeze. The more they smelled it, the more they recognized what it was. As it happened, the Sheriff was still there, and he also recognized the aroma - corn mash cooking! This proved to be the undoing of a rather successful moonshine operation!

In nineteen seventy, the mansion burned down. There are several accounts of how this took place. Some say it was a forest fire. Others say it was hobos, drunk and cooking on an open fire inside the old mansion. And there are some who believe it was lightning, a kind of vengeance caused by restless ghosts of the old jail.

Louie's Truck

Louie always carried so much junk in the back of his truck that his dog, Bo, hardly had a place to sit. Whenever Sue Ellen, his wife, would ask him when he was gonna clean out all that junk in the back of the truck, he'd look at her in surprise and say, "What junk?" She was so embarrassed to be seen riding in it, she'd walk clean into town whenever she needed something.

Now Louie was real good about hauling off the trash. The only problem Sue Ellen had with that was that he'd usually come home with more stuff than he had left with. Those dumpsters were full of "good stuff", he'd claim. He always carried a potato rake so he could lean over the sides of the dumpsters and go through the contents. He saved wire, aluminum cans, boards, furniture ...anything he thought he might use one day. Trouble was, when he wanted something out of the back of the truck, he could never find it, things were piled up so high. So it would sit right there, piling up and piling up, so he'd have to drive real slow going around corners to keep it from shifting.

Elmer and Dorman, who worked down at the filling station, had a running bet on how long it would take Louie to run out of room.

"What you gone do with all that stuff in the back of yer truck, Louie," asked Elmer one day.

Louie looked at it for a while then said, "It's all good stuff. I hate to get rid of any of it. Soon as I do, I'll end up needin' that very thing."

Well, that night they came up with a plan. They'd caught a rat snake in the barn that afternoon and put it in an old drum. They decided they'd sneak around to Louie's and put it in the back of his truck. Louie hated snakes. When he saw it, he'd have to take everything out to catch it and get rid of it.

"We shoulda come up with that a year ago. Sue Ellen's done wore out three pairs of shoes!" they laughed as they left.

Sure enough, the next morning Louie saw it curled up under a piece of an old swing set. But instead of pulling everything out of the back of his truck, he ran into the house and got his

11

shotgun. By the time he finally killed the snake, he'd also shot out all the tires and most of the windows.

Later on, Elmer and Dorman were sitting down at the filling station feeling bad because they'd made Louie do that. "I shore didn't think Louie would go crazy like that," moaned Elmer.

"Neither one of us is gonna win that bet," added Dorman.

Next thing they knew, here came Louie in a brand new truck. Sue Ellen sat right up next to him and Bo had the whole back to himself. "Guess I done kilt my truck along with that snake," Louie explained.

"We shore are sorry about that, Louie, but this here's a fine lookin' truck!" Elmer said. "Shore is!" added Dorman. "Where you headed now?"

"First thing I'moan do is haul off the trash," said Louie happily as Sue Ellen winced. "I got room for lots of stuff now!"

Christmas Lights

Fred perched himself precariously on the top of the ladder, trying to reach a nail in the eave of his house. One of his hands held a string of Christmas lights, and the other he used for balance. When the lights were secured, he gingerly backed down the ladder, and moved it to the next corner of his house. Lanier, his wife, stood out in the road surveying his handiwork.

"Fred, I see a bulb out over there," she commented. He nodded, and moved the ladder back to the last corner and slowly climbed up. He pulled out the dead bulb and inserted another, which spluttered and blinked for a moment before going out, too. He extracted that one and tried another. Gratefully, he watched it blaze into life and stay. Again, he backed down the ladder. Then the phone rang.

"I'll be right back," Lanier yelled as she ran inside to answer it. Fred sat on the third step of the ladder and lit a cigarette.

He smoked it leisurely, thankful for the break. After a few minutes, he lit another. "Where's she at?" he muttered to himself, anxious to get the job over with. Pretty soon Lanier came back out and stood in the road, eyeing the Christmas lights critically.

"Pull it up a little on that side over there," she insisted. Reluctantly, he climbed back up the ladder and began to adjust the string of lights. "That's better," she commented as he moved the ladder around to the other side of the house.

He got the strand adjusted to suit Lanier and was just starting to climb back down the ladder, when the whole display went out.

"Dern it, Fred, you musta knocked something loose," Lanier shouted. He felt a headache beginning to come on as he hiked up his overalls and lit another cigarette.

"Aren't you going to git back up there and check those connections?" asked Lanier.

"Yup. Just as soon as I finish this here cigarette," replied Fred.

"Well, if you'd stop smoking them dern cancer sticks, we could git something done around here," she commented irritably.

13

Lanier moved a plastic Santa Claus around, and fidgeted with the icicles on the outdoor Christmas tree. "Come on, Fred, we ain't got all day," she fussed.

Fred put his cigarette out and climbed back up the ladder. What he didn't know was that there was a possum hole right under the ladder, and it was beginning to cave in. The phone rang again, and Lanier started inside to answer it. "I'm outta cigarettes. Bring me that pack on top of the T.V.," he hollered as she went in the door.

He had got the lights working again and was just starting back down the ladder when the possum hole gave way. As the ladder was falling out from under him, he lunged forward and grabbed the edge of the roof. "Lanier...Lanier!" he shouted as he dangled in midair. Lanier, who was still talking on the telephone, heard him yelling frantically.

"Is somebody calling you?" asked the person on the other end of the line.

"Yes. It's Fred. He wants his dern cigarettes. Let him holler," she replied. "It'll do him good to quit smoking for a while."

Wild Man Road

He was first seen in the early sixties. Hair all wild and black. Seen running through the thick underbrush and looking back to see if you were after him. I saw him at least twice, myself. Most folks back in those days thought he looked mean and dangerous. I thought he looked scared.

Some older boys went way out there in the woods trying to spot him one time. They ended up finding a campsite. They saw where he had gotten a fire going and had cooked some squirrels. There was some moss and pine straw piled up nearby. Looked like it might have been his bed. As far as we knew, he never came into town.

One night in particular, I remember. The sky was fire-gold and lavender right before sundown. Now in those days, the main thing there was to do in our small southern town was ride around. Having plenty of dirt roads to travel, and gas being cheap, we'd load up a car full. We'd already been by old Mr. Moses and gotten some beer when we got to Wild Man Road. The ditches on each side were filled with rainwater from yesterday's downpour. We took a slippery clay-bottom turn a little too fast and found ourselves stuck in a muddy hole. No one got hurt, thank goodness. Just shook up and scared to be stranded out there in the dark ...... possibly with a wild man nearby.

There was only one thing to do, of course - walk back to town. Frogs were croaking so loud it filled up your head. Mosquitoes found us right away, so we walked even faster. The moon had risen up clear and round over the trees. None of us dared talk...the wild man might hear us!

Then, the real tingly feeling you get when you get real scared came over me. I thought I heard footsteps nearby. Then we saw him! He stood watching us for a moment. His hair stood way out and was pitch black. A long dark beard hung down over his raggedy shirt. In one hand, he had a large turtle by the neck. In the other, a long club. Something stuck out of one pants pocket. We screamed - he dropped everything and ran! Well, we ran, too - all the way back to town!

It didn't take long to round up a truck to haul us out. We just told everybody in Ada's Big Oak Restaurant what had happened. There were plenty of volunteers! We went real slow going back, looking for the wild man. Never saw him though. I never saw him again after that, but the stories went on for years. You could tell some of them were made up.

The thing that sticks in my mind is what did happen that night when we went back to pull the car out. As I said, we drove real slow. We found the spot where he dropped his club and that dead turtle (his supper, I'm sure). Right there laying in the wet clay-mud next to those things, was his tattered, dog-eared Bible.

Selling Eggs

"When dog fennel blooms, it'll be six weeks till cold weather," said Ma Bert. "Hit ain't even thought about bloomin' yet," Dora observed. "Ever year I got to listen to you moanin' about the heat," Ma Bert pointed out. "Hit ain't never bin this hot before," replied Dora. "Why, shore it has. Last year you could throw an egg up in the air and it'd be cooked before it come down," laughed Ma Bert.

Dora and Ma Bert were best friends. They were some kin, but neither of them knew exactly what. Dora was tall and husky. She had graying black hair twisted up in a tight little knot in back of her head. She lived with her husband , Fred, in the house two doors down.

Ma Bert had always lived in this rambling wooden house with the big front porch and lots of chickens in the yard. She was short, pot-bellied, and had kinky white hair that stood up right on top of her head. She had never married and was a confirmed old maid. She sold chickens and eggs for a living, and had an egg route, delivering fresh eggs to folks around town.

Dora finished off her ice tea and set her glass down beside the rocking chair. "I been thinkin'...." she began. "Don't strain yerself," muttered Ma Bert. "....ever since it got so hot I ain't felt like goin' down to the dimestore to see if they got any new dresses in," Dora continued.

"Seems to me you got plenty of dresses. How come you ain't wore that blue one with the red flowers I like so much?" asked Ma Bert. "Honey, that thing's gotten so tight I busted the buttons right off it," replied Dora. "Let's go downtown and see. I need some more brown thread anyways," suggested Ma Bert.

When they got to the dimestore, the clerk (who was an elderly woman known for her gin habit) was fast asleep in a chair beside the cash register. Her glasses had slid down her nose and fallen into her lap. She was snoring loudly. "Wisht I had me a job like that," declared Ma Bert.

While they were looking at dresses, Emma Jean Johnson came in. Emma Jean kept her hair dyed flame red and curled up in a little shelf all around her head. And she was the biggest gossip in town. In fact, folks said that if something happened on the other side of town, Emma Jean would know it before it got to the middle.

"Gained a little weight, Dora?" she asked.

"My dress size ain't none a your business," Dora replied.

Emma Jean pretended to study the goldfish display, mentally memorizing the dress size Dora was looking at. Ma Bert noticed this and decided to have a little fun. She wandered over to the men's wear section and began to hold up men's briefs.

"Come 'ere, Dora. He'll like these," she called as she held up a pair of red ones. Dora caught the wink that came and went instantaneously.

Emma Jean began to pay closer and closer attention to what they were doing. Ma Bert moved over to the lingerie department, and began to look at frilly little nightgowns. Dora followed her lead and began to really ham it up.

"Hit's about time you got yerself a man!" she commented loudly. Emma Jean almost lost her composure at this announcement. She watched closely as they woke the sleeping clerk and paid for some very suggestive items - including a bottle of Midnight in Paris perfume and some tangerine colored lipstick.

When they left, Emma Jean hurried down to the drugstore, her red shelf bobbing all around her head. "You'll never guess what I jest found out," she announced. "Ma Bert's done got herself a feller!"

By the next day, everyone had heard about the mysterious boyfriend and were thinking up excuses to buy eggs, or a fryer for supper. By the end of the week, Ma Bert had sold more than she usually did in a month. At night, she'd pull down the shades and turn up the phonograph. Folks would walk by and crane their necks trying to see through the shades. Ma Bert was having herself a ball! She wore the tangerine lipstick and fixed her hair so it wouldn't stick up in the middle. Women would drop by claiming to be making a casserole or deviled eggs. They'd hint around, trying to get her to talk about her new beau.

Finally, the rumor died out. Another one replaced it, and

folks got sick of eating chicken and eggs. "Dadgone it, Dora, I'm tired of bacon. I want a big plate of chicken and dumplins and some scrambled eggs," Ma Bert complained. "You done solt 'em all. If you eat them biddies, you will be in a mess," replied Dora. "I hope you learnt yore lesson about startin' rumors in this town!" she continued.

"Yeah," Ma Bert cackled....raise the price of eggs first!"

Solid Ground

Over here in Yellow Pine you can feel the ground shake every time a semi rolls by on the Valdosta highway. Outside my house, there's an old pump pipe sticking up out of the concrete slab. It's stuck way down into that underground river where the fresh water flows. That water is full of iron, which comes from the clay vein under the sand.

Daddy found that well. Found it with a forked stick. There are some that can still do that. Later on, when they moved the pump to a different location, Daddy found the water again. "Works every time!" he declared triumphantly, holding up the branch for us to admire.

The old pump house sat there for years, until we finally tore it down, leaving the pipe exposed. Then one year, it rained all summer long. I was outside, digging gladiola bulbs and heard this swooshing sound. The wind wasn't blowing, so I figured I'd left the kitchen sink running. Ran inside to turn it off, and realized it was coming from that old pump pipe. Daddy said, "Don't worry, it's just that underground river roaring!" We shined a flashlight down there, but couldn't see anything. Later on, the next door neighbor came across the street, asking me what that swooshing sound was.

In the mid-eighteen hundreds, this was a flat prairie. There was a sawmill, a brickyard, and two large springs. Then, one night after a long, hard rain, the ground began to shake and fall in. Folks who lived nearby thought it might be the end of the world, but it was just a couple of sinkholes falling in.

The underground river flooded, eating away at the limestone roof, until it just couldn't hold the weight on top. The sawmill was the first to go. Then the brickyard caved in. When the mill hands came to work the next morning, therewas no sawmill there - just a big pond. So they named it Mill Pond. And when the brickyard workers came to work, they also found a pond. So they named it Brickyard Pond.

21

Every time I get delusions about standing on solid ground, we'll have a good hard rain. And that underground river will start to roar.

The Peanut Man

Been scared of log trucks ever since they told me how the peanut man lost his legs. Logs came loose and rolled off, crushing both legs. Had to be amputated. Lucky to be alive, they said. Me, I wasn't all that sure.

'He used to sit up under that big oak tree downtown. Right across from the Coca Cola sign on the drugstore wall, which is still there. Had two goats to pull his cart - Claude and Maude. They always seemed to be chewing something and looking around at all us crazy humans. Boiled peanuts in little brown bags filled the front of his cart. Ten cents a bag,. Behind those peanuts was a croaker sack and a stack of paper cups for your peanut hulls. He sat propped up in the seat with his overalls tucked under him. Had tobacco stains down his front and would spit frequently into a large tin can. We all had an idea what was under the croaker sack, each one different. In fact, there was a quarter bet riding on that information!

I had completed third grade that year and was out for the summer. This was before everyone had T.V.s and it was easy for a kid to get bored. I had leaned up against a cool brick wall, downtown, one summer afternoon, listening to the old men talk. They would sit on a long wooden bench, chew tobacco, sip Coca Colas and gossip. It was a good way to find out what was going on around town!

After a while, they all left. Wasn't anybody there but me and the peanut man. This was my big chance to ask him what was under that sack! Came up and looked at him, but couldn't say a word.

"What you lookin' at? Ain't never seen nobody without no legs before?" I felt bad then, and looked down at my dirty bare feet, glad to have them. He looked away, but I didn't budge. Finally, he told me I could sit up on the seat next to him. He didn't say much, except to ask me what my name was and who my Mama and Daddy was. Then he gave me a bag of peanuts for free, which was a good thing, 'cause I didn't have ten cents.

Twice I thought about asking him what was under that croaker sack, but didn't have nerve enough. Some of them said it was a big pile of money. He would go down to the bus station every afternoon and sell peanuts to those that were getting off or on the bus. In fact, whenever it was time for the bus, Claude and Maude would look arouind at the peanut man, ready to go. This is where he sold most of his peanuts. You could always count on them having just the right amount of salt in them.

Finally, he looked over at me and said, "Ain't it about time for you to be gittin' on home?" I said I reckoned not, but could tell that it aggravated him some. Truth is, I was still trying to get my nerve up. That's when he showed me how he could spit accurately. There was a big black bug on one of Maude's ears. She had shaken it several times, trying to get it off.

"Watch this!" he grinned. Sure enough, he hit that bug dead center! Maude looked around appreciatively.

Directly, he began to get jittery. Then he looked me right in the eye and turned around and reached for the croaker sack. I began to imagine what that quarter would feel like in my pocket! He got one of those paper cups and filled it from an old milk jug under the sack. You could tell by the smell what it was. Took a few sips and let out a big sigh. Then he looked over and winked at me, as a signal not to tell. Wishing otherwise, I silently promised not to.

Costa's Cats

Eastpoint, Florida, has always been a haven for cats. This is due, in part, to the many seafood packing houses that line the waterfront. It's also due to the gentle nature of those rough looking characters in white rubber boots who supply the packing houses. It's not unusual to see pelicans, sea gulls, cats and crabs chowing down from the same piles of fishheads and assorted goodies that abound behind those packing houses. There's one fellow in particular, an oysterman by trade, who never fails to amaze me with his latest feline acquisitions.

One day, I was visiting and spotted an entire litter of kittens under the midsection of his trailer. A multitude of tails twitched and eyes narrowed, as I made my way through the hanging nets and boat parts. Going up the front steps, I had to step over a large orange and yellow tom, who didn't see fit to move out of the way. A sleek gray tabby watched me suspiciously from the porch railing. A smaller version of the tabby played under her on the porch railing, pursuing lizards and insects.

After visiting Costa and family for a while, he told me he had something to show me. He emerged from a back room holding a beautiful, long-haired, snow-white cat. Her eyes were a deep chestnut/green. She purred and seemed to smile up at him as he held her.

"She's magnificent!" I said admiringly.

"She caught three mice last week," he boasted.

"A good hunter, too," I commented.

"But that ain't the best thing about her," he said.

"What's that?" I asked.

"Well," he grinned, "she's going to have KITTENS!"

The Next Best Thing to Flying

It was an unusually cool September afternoon. Seagulls screamed overhead and I gazed up at them, wishing I could fly, too. They soared away happily as I cursed the gravity that held me here. In frustration, I decided to go for a walk, feeling earthbound and limited.

Chose an old fire trail leading to the bay. It wound through gnarled oaks framed in yellow by seaside goldenrod. Small brown birds darted here and there, reminding me of my dilemma. The air was fragrant with cedarbush.

Just on the other side of a pine grove lay the bay. It mumbled and grumbled about in its strange liquid tones. And there among the weeds was a boat. It was half buried in sand and muck. Large gaping holes stared back at me like hollow eyes.

I sat down on the grass beside the boat, wondering where it had come from. Wondering who had culled oysters on the ancient, broken cull board. What long ago storm had washed it up here? I began to imagine floating on a blue/grey bay. So far away from shore that the houses looked like tiny little boxes in the distance. Sea smells and scarlet sunsets. Limited, still, but not earthbound. Perhaps the next best thing to flying.

Heartbreak Hotel

In Tallahassee, there used to be an old house on College Avenue called the Heartbreak Hotel. It was vintage turn of the century architecture. Two storied, with dark, elegant stairway and bannister, an ample kitchen and pantry. Florida State University was only a few bloocks away.

This grand old neighborhood had given way to demand for student housing by the nineteen sixties. By the seventies, the Heartbreak Hotel was inhabited mainly by students, artists, writers, musicians, and craftsmen. Each one seemed to add a personal touch. Poems and artwork on doors and walls, intricately designed shelves and furniture, a private sundeck atop the roof, a most unusual apartment built into the space under the house. There was no end to its mysteries and delights. Creativity thrived during those years.

In the yard, you were likely to see such things as an old motorcycle painted pink, decorated lavishly with lace; something that looked like an elephant leaning up against a tree, assortments of sparkling geodes and rocks, pineapple mint and yarrow beds, or a macrame creation. Music ranged from totally unstructured to classical and could be heard at practically any hour. Heartbreak seems to inspire greatness in creative people. A lot of the residents there had recently lost out on love, gravitating naturally to the bosom of the Heartbreak Hotel. Plus, the rent was cheap.

Many folks came and went during those years, some finally achieving fame. Oddly enough, the Heartbreak Hotel was sold the day Elvis died, in August, 1977. It was torn down a year later to make room for a parking lot. At times you can still smell the pineapple mint or see a small white yarrow blossom peeping up from in between the concrete slabs.

Elbert and the Worms

Elbert was a worm grunter, who grew up around Blountstown. To be a worm grunter, you have to go way out into the woods and stick a stob down into the ground. Then you run a stick over it to make it buzz. This makes the worms wiggle up close to the surface. Then you just dig them up, carry them to the fishing supply store, and sell them. Elbert made some good money doing that.

One day Elbert went a little bit farther out into the woods than usual. And ran across a still. There were several jugs of moonshine sitting around and Elbert thought he'd just have one tiny little sip. Well, that sip tasted so good, he decided he'd carry the jug along with him.

Later on, when he first went to grunting, he decided to have another little sip. Then another, and another. Finally, Elbert got drunk and accidentally knocked over the jug of moonshine. It spilled out all over the ground around where he was grunting up worms. But instead of moving to a fresh area, he just stayed right there and kept on grunting.

Finally, when he'd gotten a couple of buckets full, he passed out. He slept and slept. When he woke up, his head felt dizzy and he was real, real thirsty. So he grabbed those buckets of worms and headed to the fishing supply store.

By the time he got there, the worms had all died off from alcohol poisoning. Elbert felt so bad he didn't even notice they had stopped wriggling. He just grabbed four Coca Colas and drank them down as fast as he could.

Then he handed his buckets to the store owner and sat down on a bench. The fellow took one look at those worms and handed them back. "I can't buy these worms!" he said. "They're all dead!"

Elbert just shook his throbbing head, opened up another Coca Cola, and replied, "No sir - they're just dead drunk!"

Ten Miles To Telogia

The sun was so hot, I thought my head was going to explode like a ripe cantaloupe. The sign said ten miles to Telogia, and my chances of getting a ride looked worse and worse. I had left out of Carrabelle early that morning, when it was cool, expecting to hitch a ride right away. The only two cars that had passed me so far had not even slowed down to look me over. I switched my bag to my left hand, because the right one was beginning to cramp.

On either side of me were muddy ditches. Beyond that was palmetto and pine scrub. Here and there, I passed swampy areas. Snakes were so thick in these areas I couldn't get near the water. Humidity caused steam to rise from the asphalt, and clouds loomed in threatening gray formations overhead. Thunder menaced in the distance. If it rained, there was nowhere to go for cover, unless I made my way through sharp-edged palmetto brush. Rattlesnakes were fond of curling up under the fan-like leaves, and did not take kindly to being disturbed. I picked up my pace - hoping to come to a house or some other kind of shelter.

Instead, I came to a bog. Mosquitoes and yellow flies attacked me immediately. I began to run, wildly slapping them away from my face. Suddenly, a large brown moccasin darted into my path. I barely missed stepping on it by at least an eighth of an inch! Then I stopped completely.

A huge bull 'gator blocked the road. He turned and stared at me... all fifteen feet of him! His tail began to swish and he snorted loudly. I found my feet and turned and ran, feeling his breath on my heels.

A pothole tripped me and I fell, sprawling, on the searing asphalt. The 'gator was closing in, his jaws open for the kill. As he lunged for me, I rolled over and over, finally falling into a slimy ditch.

A truck came barreling by at that very minute. Its muffler was missing and it sounded like a freight train. The 'gator ran off into the woods on the other side of the road. I raised up and tried to flag them down, but they were already gone.

At least I was still alive, but my bag was gone. I must have dropped it somewhere along the road in my mad dash for survival. So once again, I began to trudge those last ten miles to Telogia. And that's when it started to rain.

It came down faster and faster. The wind was howling and lightning was making bright streaks across the darkened sky. Once again, I began to run. Soon I came to a small dirt side road. Thinking that perhaps a house might be down there, I turned in.

There was no house, but an old rusted-out car stood beside the weedy road. I tried to open the door, but it was stuck, so I climbed through the broken window, slashing my jeans and ripping my shirt. Blasts of lightning struck like bombs. The rain was torrential, running in rivers off the top of the car. Wearily, I settled in. Any refuge was better than none. Or so I thought.

A jab of pain ended my short nap. Then another. And another. Wasps! The old car was filled with wasps! I dove out the window, almost cutting my jugular vein. And ran back out onto the highway. Drenched to the bone, I pressed onward to Telogia.

Eventually, the rain stopped. My ankle was hurting and beginning to swell. I must have twisted it when I tripped in the pothole. Up ahead was a large shady oak tree standing beside the road. I limped over to it and sat down, leaning against its massive trunk.

As I gazed upward into the branches, something large caught my eye. It was a fat possum, moving slowly across a large, black limb. With horror I realized that the limb was rotten! The stupid possum continued to climb outward on the limb. A loud cracking noise brought me to my feet! Then the limb fell.

Once again I dashed back onto the road. The limb had missed me, but the small outer branches scratched my face and the top of my head. Feeling lucky to be alive again, I trudged northward. Soon a sign came into view. It said two miles to Telogia. I was almost there!

The afternoon sun blazed hotter and hotter. Why had I not thought to catch some of the rainwater and drink it? Those last few miles seemed like a thousand, at that point. But I stoically hobbled along.

Like a mirage, the roofs of Telogia began to appear in the distance. I was almost there! If it hadn't been for the twisted ankle, I would have begun to run again. It was then that I heard the car. It passed me, slowed down, backed up, and someone yelled.

"Hey, buddy! Need a ride?"

Square Sponges

During the first part of this century, sponge fishing still provided a living for a lot of folks. Greek immigrants in the North Florida area brought their knowledge and skill at sponge fishing from the old country. In Gulf waters, from Cedar Key to Apalachicola, bath sponges grew in abundance.

During Prohibition (1920s) a young man from Perry became friendly with some local Greek sponge fishermen. He had a great love of the sea and wanted very much to accompany them on one of their fishing expeditions. They were reluctant at first, but he finally talked them into it.

Now in those days, the road from Perry to Keaton Beach was no more than a sandy, two-rut trail through the scrub oaks and cabbage palms. Wild hogs and rattlesnakes thrived in the region.

They left early the next morning while it was still dark, driving a truck filled with wooden crates to transport the fresh catch. As they neared the beach, the smell of the ocean grew stronger and the young man could hardly wait to get to the water.

When they arrived, they put the boat in and rowed out aways. Then they stuck a glass bottomed bucket down into the surf in order to scan the bottom. When a clump of sponges was sighted, one of the men would reach down into the water with a long sponge hook while the rest of the party steadied the boat. Later on, when it began to get hot, they dove the sponges up. This went on for some time, and the boat began to get full. Then a strange thing happened.

The man with the glass bottomed bucket cried, "Square sponge!" and the other men began laughing, whooping and talking excitedly in Greek. Two of the men jumped overboard and returned to the surface with a square wooden box. They put it under the sponges in the middle of the boat. Not long after that, it happened again. Every time, the man with the bucket would yell, "Square sponge!" and the rest would shout with joy. By this time, the young man was really curious as to what was in those boxes. He found out when they went to unload the boat.

After forming a line from the truck to the boat, they began to pass crates along to be filled with sponges. Then they'd pass them on back to the truck when they were full. The first heavy crate caught the young man by surprise. It was twice as heavy as the rest. He dropped it into the soft sand and heard a clinking sound.

The Greek men ran over and pulled off the top layer of sponges in the crate. There, on the bottom, was one of the square wooden boxes. The men pried a few boards off the top and looked down inside. The "square sponge" was filled with long brown bottles labeled...'Puerto Rico - Fine Rum!'

The Night We Saw Fairies

I must record these events as accurately as possible. It has been many years and memory does not seem to improve with age. My companions on this night have long since lost touch. I wonder sometimes if they remember, too.

We were all students - Kristin, Patty and I. During the day we went to our respective Universities, and at night, worked in the same restaurant. Indeed, we were treated more like members of the family than mere employees. Perhaps it was this atmosphere that lent itself to the loyal camaraderie of us waitresses. It was a night of muffled laughter, due to the fact that one of our fellow food servers had come to work under the influence of Quaaludes (a popular recreational drug at the time.)

Patty lived in one of the most scenic and unspoiled regions of the now metropolitan area. Her apartment was part of an old plantation home that was surrounded by Japanese persimmons, azaleas, and camellias. It stood majestically on the apex of a high hill, overlooking acres and acres of green pasture land. The setting was almost surreal. "Let's party at my place," said Patty. "Tonight there's a full moon."

We got off work about 10:30 and headed to the Junior Food Store across the street for a six-pack of Rolling Rock beer. High energy propelled us, filling us with song and laughter. The cashier was not amused as we serenaded him with "Good Night, Irene" on the way out. Patty flipped him the bird.

Kristin was a talented young actress from Sarasota. Her face was angelically pretty and she sang with style and assurance. Patty was a serious dance student with a finely toned body that wouldn't wait. I was studying flute, and had just acquired a coin-silver, French open-hole model. It was sweet. We three were fond of impromptu flute, voice and dance ensembles, performing often in parking lots and public bathrooms.

We worked ourselves into an hysterical surge of laughter re-iterating the events of our work night. Linda (the drug impaired waitress) had kept running into a fake fireplace in the middle of the dining room, with her serving cart. It was loaded with a huge

Chateaubriand, and the fire kept going out every time she bumped it. She had also flung out a whole plate of spaghetti into a woman's open purse that she had left sitting beside her chair. No one saw it happen but us. The entire serving had sailed off the plate like a frisbee and landed neatly into the open jaws of the large brown handbag. We were speculating the possibility that maybe she wouldn't find it for hours or even days!

We ran toward the crab-apple trees, pink and aromatic in Spring moonlight. "Did you know that today is the Spring Equinox?" Kristin asked with a smile. Of course! Spirits of Nature had called us to pasture! We ran far down the hill to the right of the house, where mushrooms shone beigely in moonlight.

I put my flute together. Melodies flowed easily and seemed to weave a spell over my friends as the dance began. Leaping and twirling, they moved liquidly over grass and clover.

Kristin looked over at Patty and started to giggle. We did, too, caught up in the silliness supreme. Then we saw what she was giggling about! Three tiny people sat on a toadstool watching us! Their wings glittered and gleamed, and they had tiny silver antennae over their eyes. They were dressed in silky dresses and there was a bright white aura around them. Their hair was long and curly and they had large purple eyes.

Suddenly it was as if the music was playing me! The tiny creatures flew overhead, sprinkling us with luminescent dust. We rose slowly, almost imperceptibly at first, into the air. Just when I thought it would go on forever, a light appeared in the sky. It grew steadily brighter, and I realized it was the sun coming up. Slowly we danced now, finally collapsing onto wet grass. The fairies blew us kisses and disappeared.

The sun rose, casting slanted rays of light onto magical pastures. We had been blessed. "Spring Equinox, huh?" laughed Patty. We began to giggle again, loudly enough for echoes to ring. "I think I'm sleepy," yawned Kristin as she started for the house. Patty followed her. I sat for a while, too exhausted to sleep. The sun was hovering above treetops when I felt myself start to doze off. I stood up and stretched, then bent down to pick up my flute. We had danced a circle, neatly worn down, in the grass. And there, in the middle of the circle, lay a piece of glass, or something that reflected light. I knelt down and picked it up. It was a piece of fairy dress, made of a material so sheer and shimmery I thought it must be spun gold and silver. I wrapped it in a piece of tin foil back at the house.

Recently all this was brought back to mind as I was going through some things in the attic. In the bottom of a large box marked 'Tallahassee - 1976', I found it, still wrapped in tin foil. It was in the carved Indian box I kept my jewelry in many years ago. Just a tiny little piece of some exquisite material that a fairy had worn to dance in once upon a time

A Fishing Story

Mr. Bishop liked to fish. He was one of those kind that can sit still in one place for hours - waiting for a fish to come by. One day, we were anchored right in the middle of the Aucilla River, when Fred, his dog, began to bark. Looked around to the back of the boat, and there was the biggest dern moccasin I'd ever seen. Had a head on him like a football! Guess it had come after the fish in our bucket.

"That snake comes up ever time I git a few stumpknockers," he said.

"You know this snake?" I asked.

"Yup," he answered. "First time he come up was in '65." By this time I had a feeling Mr. Bishop was going to pull my leg.

"Yup. Early summer it was. Heard a noise back there in the back of the boat, turned around, and there he was. Had one of my fish in his mouth already," he began. I was still eyeballing that snake which was swimming off by now.

"Reckon you didn't shoot him, if that's the same one," I said.

"Nope. I'd been sitting there all morning waiting for one of those stumpknockers to come by so I could catch them. It sorta teed me off. I had to figure out a way to make that snake let go and swim off. Bein' as how I had me a full beer at the time, I just eased down there and poured that ice cold Miller on 'im. Well, it worked. Then I seen him a few months later - right here in the same spot. Critter was after my fish again. Seeing as how the first time worked, I figgered I'd try it again. Sure enough, it did. Same thing happened last year. Reckon he didn't find no fish today, cause we ain't caught none." Mr. Bishop laughed.

About that time, we heard a knocking on the side of the boat. Both of us looked down, and there was the snake looking up - with a fish in his mouth!

Louis Hill

Louis Hill is said to be one of the finest moonshiners that ever lived in North Florida. Folks were known to come from as far away as the Carolinas to purchase his wares. He lived in the woods on the south side of Madison County. Down there close to the San Pedro Swamp. Although he had occasional brushes with the law, he managed to keep on brewing his famous 'shine.

His wife was named Anna, and they had a girl named Ruby Merle. Everybody called the girl Sugar Babe. Louis was a husky man, with long hair and a beard. He always wore bib overalls and boots, and he rode a big red horse. They lived in a ramshackle house with a tin roof and a front porch. He kept cows in the woods and lots of chickens at his house. It is said that they roosted so often on the porch that there were stalgmites of chicken manure under the eaves where the rain couldn't get to them.

Inside the house, there was a trunk in the back room. It contained two gallons of fine moonshine. For one dollar, he'd fill up your glass and your bottle. When he wasn't home, Anna would attend to business.

There's one story about Louis and Anna going downtown to see the new furniture store in town. They walked around, admiring all the fancy furniture; but what caught Louis' eye was the piano. It was the style of the day to have a piano in your parlor. He turned around and asked his wife, "You want a piana?"

To which she replied, "Nope - I did afore I left the house!"

Their two gravestones standside by side under an oak tree in the middle of the San Pedro cemetery. He passed away six months after she did, in April, 1962.

Sugar Babe died in childbirth, the house was eventually torn down, and Louis' gravestone has crumbled into pieces. Perhaps the only thing that remains intact is the legend.

Wolf Rats

There was something strange going on at those dog farms. Nobody would tell me what it was at first. In fact, if you asked they'd look away and act like they didn't hear you. Made me wonder. Then I heard that some neighbors were mad because the dogs kept them awake at night. I get off work at the packing plant at twelve thirty, six nights a week, and have to drive past three of those dog farms to get home. Sometimes I'll hear them raising enough Cain to wake the dead down there in the Macedonia graveyard! I used to stop and look around and try to figure out what made them go crazy like that. Never did see anything wrong. Figured they were barking just to be barking.

Then one Sunday afternoon I went fishing. Met this old man down there sitting in my fishing spot. We went to talking and I found out he lived right there on one of those dog farms. First, he didn't want to talk about it. Said they run a clean kennel. Later on, he began to talk about those greyhounds. Said they were a high-strung type of dog. Said he could tell by the bark what they were saying.

"One night," he went on, "they was makin' such a racket I couldn't do nothin' to quiet 'em. So I went and got my big flashlight and my gun. Turned my light on in that first pen., and there was the biggest dern rat I ever seen! Them wharf rats over by the St. John's River ain't half as big as this thing was! By the time I could take aim, he was gone down a hole he'd dug. That hole was so big you could fit a hog in there!" This got my attention.

A week or so later, I was down at the store getting me a Fireball or two and ran into this woman I knew that ran one of those dog farms. Asked her straight out about those rats.

"Them things is gettin' to be a problem. I been in the dog business for a long time and I ain't never seen nothin' like this until about a year ago," she said. "Every now and then they'll burrow up under the dog pens and eat all the dog food. That's probably how they got so derned big. They'll finish the last little bit of the tunnel at night when everythings quiet and dark. I've stayed up nights trying to shoot one, but they're quick! We've took to guardin' our puppies, as a few have disappeared. We call 'em Wolf Rats!"

Not long after that, I was gassing up my truck and ran into someone else I knew that had a dog farm.

"We'd done bought ourselves a brand new double-wide when we run into 'em last time," he said. "We was movin' our old trailer to the back lot for Myrtle Lou and the kids. And derned if that trailer didn't bog down in one a them Wolf Rat tunnels. I was so mad, I was gonna crawl up in there with my gun, but I finally come to my senses. We dug the trailer up and got it moved, then come back with the shovels -- gonna dig them rats out! It cain't be done in a day's time! Guess they was tired of dog food and was comin' after somethin' in our trailer."

Last night I gave Uncle Dave a ride home from work, as his truck is broke down. We passed by one of those dog farms and heard those greyhounds raising one heck of a fuss. "What do you reckon they're barking at?" I asked him.

"Nothin'," he replied. "Them dogs is just barkin' to be barkin'."

Valentine Day Story

He retired from his job as a truck driver in order to stay home and tend to his dying wife. It was a hard time for him, but he figured he'd make the most of their remaining time together. He faithfully tended her flower garden, which had been planted lavishly with bright varieties in order to attract butterflies. She would sit on her bench and watch them as they went from flower to flower.

He had even built her some small cages to hold caterpillars, so they could watch the cocoons being built and the new butterflies hatch. Then they'd let them loose and watch as the graceful insects glided through the garden, feasting on nectar.

When she went to the hospital, he decorated her room with pictures of butterflies. He even surprised and delighted the hospital staff by bringing in one of the caterpillar cages so everyone could watch the new butterflies hatch.

One day, he arrived to find her slipping away. He knew that this would be the last time they could be together, so he sat by her bedside just holding her hand. "Is the cardinal vine blooming yet?" she asked. "Everything is blooming and your garden is full of butterflies," he responded. "Be sure and water when the dry season comes," she said as her breathing became shallower. "I'm going to miss you so much," he told her, barely controlling his grief.

"I'll always be with you. You'll see," she said, as she breathed her last.

In order to overcome his loneliness and depression, he took to the high seas. He bought a boat for off-shore fishing and spent most of the next year far, far away from land. The solitude and beauty of the Gulf brought him confort in his time of mourning.

One afternoon as he sat watching the waves and cumulus clouds, he realized that today was Valentine's Day, the day he had married. This made him miss her so terribly, he felt like throwing himself overboard so he could drown in the blue/green depths.

He put his head in his hands and wept out the tears he had been holding back all this time. When he raised his eyes he saw something small and colorful skipping across the water. In amazement he watched the butterfly coming closer and closer. It did not waver in its course, but came straight for his boat, landing softly but firmly on his cheek.

Lucilla's Hair-Do

Lucilla was madder than Joe had ever seen her. She came home from the beauty shop with a head full of frizzy, greenish blond hair. He said how it really didn't look that bad, but he was lying. "You kin bet they didn't git none a my money for this mess on my head," she announced as she plopped herself down on the couch.

Well, this was a big mistake. One leg was gone off it, so Joe had propped up that corner with a couple of old bricks. They just couldn't take the strain anymore and picked that very minute to crumble. Next thing Lucilla knew, she was sliding toward the floor, which wasn't too good a thing, either. Evinrude, the cat, was lying right there on the floor next to the couch. Lucilla picked that very spot to land. Well, she missed Evinrude, but hit right square on the tip of his tail. Now Lucilla was a good sized woman, and she must have flattened that thing right out!

Evinrude came up off the floor yowling and scratching. Lucilla couldn't have gotten any madder right then if she'd tried to. In fact, with her face all red and her hair tinted green, she kind of looked like a Christmas ornament. But Joe knew better than to bust out laughing right then! He helped hoist her up off the floor, which was no easy job. She was definitely not a light load!

Well, she went for the bathroom. Slammed the door so hard, two pictures fell off the wall. Howard, Joe's boy, came out of his room and came over and sat down at the table with him.

"Dad, he said, "she was ugly to begin with. How you gonna live with a woman who's got green hair?"

Howard didn't like Lucilla, because she was his step-mother, Joe's second wife. The only thing he did like about her was her cooking. In fact, mealtime was the only time they really got along.

"Only thing I'm worried about," Joe said, "is how she's gonna go to work at the truck stop lookin' like she's got spruce pines growin' up outta her head." Which got Howard and Joe both to laughing.

Lucilla finally came out of the bathroom, with her hair all wet. "I been tryin' to wash this mess out," she explained. Joe knew she was upset, so he got up and got his own glass of tea. Just to be nice, he got her one, too. She began to settle down a little bit after that.

The next day Lucilla called in sick to work. Joe didn't blame her - he would have done the same thing. Then she got in the kitchen and showed out. They ate better that day than the king himself. She cooked breakfast with home-made biscuits, lunch with fresh vegetables, and supper with blueberry pie, from scratch. "Lucilla, darlin', I'm so full you won't have to cook again for three days!" Joe told her.

Lucilla just nodded her fuzzy green head and picked up another cook- book.

Well, that hair-do turned out to be a blessing. You see, she never went back to work at the truck stop. She just stayed home and kept on cooking. Howard and her got along better and better. And Joe didn't have to worry about those truck drivers making passes at her anymore.

One day, when that green hair-do had grown out some, Joe, Howard and Lucilla were sitting on the porch shelling peas. She looked at Joe and said, "You shore must love me a lot. Most men wouldn't want no woman got hair the color of duckweed."
Joe just patted his stomach, winked at Howard, and replied, "Darlin', you look good to me!"

The Hitchhiker

Kilgore took a notion one day and bought himself a guitar. He loved the sound of it and was beginning to learn a chord or two. His early years were spent in West Virginia, and he favored the hillbilly style. One night during the early nineteen twenties, he was driving his Model T from Perry to Tallahassee with the new guitar beside him on the seat. When he was only a short distance from town, he spotted a slender young man walking along the side of the lonely, dark highway. So he stopped.

"Need a ride?" he asked. The young man coughed violently for a moment, then got in. "Shore do thank you," said the stranger.

"You oughten to be walking this dusty old road with a cough like that," Kilgore observed. Then the stranger spotted the guitar.

"You play that thing, or just carry it around?" he asked.

Well, Kilgore told him to have at it, and the young man began to strum. Then he began to sing in a clear, plaintive voice. Kilgore perked up at the lively sound, feeling amazed at the quality of the music. Just when he thought it could get no better, the stranger began to yodel. Pretty soon they were both singing and talking as they rolled along.

The young musician told him that he worked for the railroad as a brakeman. Then, he sang train songs for the next few miles. Kilgore noticed that his music and conversation were sometimes punctuated by more coughing spells.

In no time at all, they reached Tallahassee. Once there, Kilgore insisted on driving him all the way to the train station. This gave him time to listen to one more song. It was a twelve-bar blues tunes called "Blue Yodel No.6", by far the best song yet.

When they reached the station, Kilgore was sorry the stranger was getting out. In fact, he invited him to visit whenever he was in the area. As he started to drive off, he stopped and yelled out the window, "What did you say your name was?" The young man looked back over his shoulder and replied..."Rodgers - Jimmie Rodgers!"

Author's footnote: Jimmie Rodgers was also known as the "singing brakeman." He is recognized as being one of the first to legitimize the country music field. He died in 1933, at age 36, from tuberculosis.

The Day I Quit!

Frost glistened on brown grass as early morning sunrays penetrated the deep forest. I was awakened by noisy first-birds. If it weren't for a few slash pines, the morning would have been entirely gray and brown. I searched through my backpack for the Camels, my wake- up ritual. They weren't there!

Must have left them in the jacket pocket. Hurriedly I checked, craving the soothing nicotine. Not there, either. After frantically looking over the whole campsite, I realized I had thrown them into the fire last night! A fitting last gesture for one so long addicted. Regretfully, I now remembered the joy I had felt at "starting anew." It was a mind set.... now lost. And it was a long hike back to the fish camp, but that's what I had to do to get a cigarette.

Shouldering backpack and sleeping bag, I set off. On cold mornings like this, my joints ached and my legs were stiff. Toes on each foot were hurting from the cold. Melting frost on my shoes had rendered both of them damp, increasing the pain. I walked faster, hoping to warm them.

At one point, I thought I was going the wrong way. It was a moment of panic. By this time, all I could think of was a lit cigarette in my hand. This was definitely not the time to get lost in a National Forest! I thought of taking a few sips of brandy to warm my innards, but that would just make me want a cigarette more. In fact, it was the brandy nightcap that had brought on this insanity of quitting tobacco! I pushed through thick underbrush, thankful that the rattlesnakes were sleeping far underground. This was not the way I had hiked in, but it was in the right direction - east.

All of a sudden, I realized I was not going forward, but down. I was in deep quicksand! Fear caused me to forget my craving, and the cold.

That's when I realized there was a rope in my backpack. Hope is a great motivator, and I became galvanized into action. There was a low limb hanging over the treacherous pool. I aimed for that. This is a problem when you're not a seasoned cowhand. My arms were just above the quicksand, but just barely, when I finally made it and pulled myself to safety. Boy, did I ever want a smoke right then to calm myself down!

After that, it was even harder going, as I was thoroughly damp. Finally, the woods began to look familiar. Then I came to a big ravine and had to ease my way down the steep earth. When I reached bottom, I noticed the damp leaves had been moved and dug around in. With horror, I saw a large wild hog approaching - faster and faster, the fury burning visibly in his primitive eyes. There was one mid-sized pine nearby, and I lunged for it. There were no lower limbs and I slid back almost as fast as I scrambled up. Finally, God knows how, I made it to a large upper branch, upon which I sat, wishing for a cigarette.

That hog began to butt the tree furiously, and I feared I might be thrown off my branch. Eventually he was pacified by the sandwiches and potato chips I threw down. With a last grunt of satisfaction, he disappeared into the underbrush. I stayed on my perch until I could no longer hear him in the bushes. Getting down proved more treacherous than getting up, as I was no longer fueled by adrenalin. About half way down I lost my grip and landed heavily on my back. Regaining your wind after a fall like that is not easy. I thought surely I would die from lack of oxygen, but gradually began to breathe normally. again. At this point, I could actually taste the burning tobacco, only to realize I was still a long way from a cigarette.

On the other side of the ravine was a flat, sandy pine forest. This made the going a lot easier until I heard the thunder. Then the sky became dark as slate. I looked up and was pelted with speeding raindrops and knocked off my feet by a blast of lightning!

The tree next to me exploded and the entire top landed not more than a foot away! Miraculously, I was unhurt. After the downpour, I was completely drenched and colder than I ever thought possible. And savagely hungry!

Unfortunately, I had thrown everything edible in my backpack down to that wild hog. The only thing left with calories in it was the brandy, which I eagerly downed, and set off again. If I had not thrown those Camels in the fire last night, none of this would have happened!

Luckily I made it back to the fish camp about dusk. I staggered into my cabin, collapsing onto the sofa. Delbert, my cabin mate, awoke from his bunk and stared at me with alarm. I was soaked to the bone and shivering. My face and arms were cut and bruised, my clothing torn and filthy. He helped me into a hot shower and some dry clothing as I wearily explained what had happened, leaving out the part about the Camels. As I finished my first meal in twenty- four hours, he thoughtfully reached into his pocket and brought out his cigarettes, and offered me one.

"No, thanks." I heard myself say. "I quit!"

Snake Man

Fall was nipping at the corners of the days. Just a tiny hint of coolness appeared in early morning and late afternoon. Dog fennel and horsetail shot upward, getting ready for bloomtime. Cicadas droned and gnats formed giant balls of moving orbs.

August was a time to remember. A time of change. Dog days were ripe with the scent of freshly mown grass and maypops in bloom. Farmers turned cornfields under and planted winter rye. Butterflies winged by in myriad colors on their long trek southward. Afternoon cumulus clouds built up in mountainous formations until they squeezed out the rain. It was nature's last burst before freezing winds and plunging temperatures turned green into brown, flowers into seed. Endless summer was coming to an end.

Nathaniel drank the last of his beer and crushed the empty can under his heel. The spring was full of people today. They sat on the sandy beach or swam in the cool aqua-blue water. Boats came and went on the river. Sometimes they'd pull up next to the spring, tying their boats onto gnarled roots below cypress and oak trees that lined the bank. Unlike most of the good springs nowadays, this one was still free and natural.

He threw the crushed can into the back of his pickup. Then he took off his shoes and got a towel from the dashboard. Children splashed and screamed in delight as he climbed down the river bank and walked around to the spring. Its icy depths mingled with warm brown river water where the two met. He sat down on a linestone boulder and looked around for familiar faces. There were none.

Across the river he saw a large brown moccasin glide gracefully to and fro. A hawk soared overhead. Nathaniel took a cigarette out of his rolled up shirt sleeve. He tapped in on the boulder, then lit it.

Later, he saw the brown water moccasin again, moving in zigzags across the river toward the spring. Several small children played in the shallow water near the tree roots. The snake swam closer and closer. Nathaniel stood up and walked over to where the children were playing. The moccasin dove under a half submerged log and disappeared. When he saw it again, it was curling around nearby roots, close to where the two little girls were building a sand castle.

He picked up a stick and moved closer. The moccasin gazed calmly into his eyes. Nathaniel stopped and gazed back. Gently, almost imperceptibly, the snake began to back down into the water.

"Look at this!" Nathaniel said as he picked up a mussel shell from the beach. The two little girls came over to see his shell. "This here's a freshwater shellfish," he told the girls as each one held the shell in amazement.

The water moccasin swam past the log and dove under.

"Here, you can have it," said Nathaniel as the children squealed appreciatively. When they returned to their sand castle, the snake was zigzagging back across the river. When it reached the other side, it looked into Nathaniel's eyes one last time before disappearing into nearby woods.

Anna Saves the Day (And the moonshine)

Once when Louis Hill was out tending to his moonshine still, his wife, Anna, received word that the revenoors were coming. Unfortunately, by the time she found this out, they were already approaching the house. Being a quick-thinking, resourceful woman, she immediately opened the trunk in the back room and removed the moonshine.

When the revenoors got there, they found the front door open, and Anna sitting in her rocking chair, furiously rocking back and forth. Since she was known to have a fiery temper, and a handy shotgun, they decided to handle this delicate situation with caution.

"You could save us a lot of trouble if you'd just show us where the shine is," said one. "Ain't no moonshine here," replied Anna, her eyes flashing. So while one of the revenoors stayed with Anna, trying to talk her into giving up the contraband, the rest of them began searching the house. Anna just rocked and glared, her long skirt billowing out around the rocking chair.

A little while later, finding nothing, they decided to give up. "You shore could make things a lot easier if you'd just hand over them moonshine jugs," demanded one of the revenoors. "Jest get up outa that rocking' chair and show us where it is. We know it's here," threatened another. Anna rocked and glared some more. Finally, empty handed and frustrated, the revenoors left. And Anna stopped rocking. She sighed a breath of relief as she removed two jugs from under her rocking chair and put them into the trunk in the back room where they belonged.

Under the House

Under the house was where we went when it was hot as blazes in the summertime. Up under there, the sand was dry and fine, like gray sugar. You could hear the water pipes creaking, and the toilet flushing. We'd get little sticks and stir up the doodle-bug holes, saying "Doodle-bug, doodle-bug, fly away home; your house is on fire and your children will burn." Then, the tiny feelers would appear, and we'd watch in wonder as the doodle-bug made its way to the surface.

Under the house was where the dogs stayed. It was cool in summer and warm in winter. Our gas heater was right in the center of the house. When it was cold, the dogs would huddle up right under where the heater was. When it rained, they stayed dry. They had their puppies under there, and kept away the snakes.

We made us a fort under the house, using old bricks and boards to designate rooms. When the grown-ups were angry, it became our hide-away.

The house was built on a slope, so that you could almost stand up and walk under the back porch. There were steep wooden stairs leading down into the yard. The back porch is where the laundry was done. It always smelled of soap and bleach. Sometimes grass would try to grow under the stairs. It stuck out from the sides and between the steps, looking white and thin.

One cold winter day, there was a terrible storm. It was late December. A cold front from the northwest came roaring across Florida, preceded by freezing rain and tornadoes. The radio crackled and squawked as the whole family listened for weather updates.

I was worried about the new puppies, seven of them, who'd been born a few days ago. My sister, my cousin and I decided we'd slip out of the house to check on them. We bundled up, got a flashlight and made our way down the back stairs. The wind was howling around us and we were chilled to the bone. Lightning flashed again and again as we made our way under the house. My cousin turned on the flashlight and we gasped in amazement at what we saw then.

Along side our dogs, snuggled up and warm as toast, were two coons, a squirrel, and a whole family of possums!

How Sopchoppy Got Started

Grandpa Stuckey sat in a straightback chair on the porch. He did that serious lean where you think he might go over any minute, but never does. "Oh, Lord!" he moaned.

This was how all our conversations got started lately.

"Feeling okay?" I asked. He had been threatening quite loudly to fall over dead any minute since it got so hot. You never knew with someone like Grandpa Stuckey --- he was real stubborn.

"Been to Sopchoppy since I was here last," I said.

"Mosquiters bad?" he asked?

"Real bad down on the river banks. Got me some catfish, though."

"Sopchoppy," he mused. "This here is what I heard about Sopchoppy. Back in the 1800s, a bunch of settlers come down from South Car'liner in covered wagons."

"Musta been hard going through woods in them days," I said.

"Dern right! Only thing they had to make do with was some huntin' dogs and a plow mule. They was alright till the mule took sick."

"What happened to him?" I questioned, so he would know I was listening.

Grandpa Stuckey took a Camel out of his shirt pocket and lit it with a "Swim Naked" lighter I had brought him from Panama City Beach.

"They tell me Sopchoppy means Black Water in Indian," I mentioned so he would remember what he was talking about.

"First that mule quit eatin'," he continued between puffs. "Then when he quit drinkin', they really got worried. They had to get some water down that mule."

He suddenly leaned forward in his chair and began shaking. "What is it," I cried in alarm, then realized he was laughing.

"Some dern fool Car'linern says 'let's put that huntin' horn up his rear and pour some water in 'im.' Well, they went to pourin'. Pretty soon that mule raised his head up offen the ground and looked around. Directly, that mule began to bunch his feet up under 'im. They bunched tighter and tighter. All of a sudden he jumped up offen the ground and lit off acrost them swamps. The first time he hit ground, that huntin' horn went off ---loud and clear! That set them huntin' dogs to howlin'. The second time he hit ground, they begun to tear loose from that wagon! After the third or fourth time, even them settlers couldn't hold 'em back. The horn-blowin' and the howlin' got fainter and fainter. Finally it begun to get dark. What settlers had tried to round 'em up just quit and went on back to camp."

"Did they ever catch them?" I giggled.

"Nope. And without that mule and them huntin' dogs, they couldn't figure out what to do next, so they just stayed right there, fishin' on that black river. That's how Sopchoppy got started!"

Calhoun Corners

I'm here to tell you about a remarkable place! Right off a dirt road going towards Pinetta. Turn left at the dumpsters. Look for the barn covered in vines, then real close to spot the driveway. Go slow. When you pull up you'll see the cars. Rambler, Plymouth, and a black Ford truck. Next to the house is the biggest sycamore tree I've ever seen. Last winter, when it was foggy and cold, that tree was full of big black buzzards. When I slammed the car door, they all flew off -- wings flapping like thunder. I took it as a sign.

Be careful going through the stickers and that pile of tin. Snakes hide up in there. When you get to the back porch, watch those first few boards, as they kinda sag.

To the left, ivy covers all. Maybe grown wild from some potted plants they used to keep. In that old shed are some lawn chairs and a fallen in table. There's what's left of the chicken pen beyond that. On your right is the bathroom. Only thing left is the sink and a few homemade shelves, carefully hand beveled and put in convenient places. There's holes for a wood burning stove.

Next on your right is the kitchen and dining room, divided by a wall with two openings. The top one has wide ledges on both sides. This is where I imagine the food was passed out.

Fried chicken, cornbread, and black-eye peas full of bacon grease. They must of sent the dirty dishes back to the kitchen on a cart through that bottom opening, as it's big enough. Outside all the windows (which have been broken) are shelves, also hand beveled. Wonder if they used to put pies out there to cool. Bet they had blackberry and peach. All this is separate from the main house.

Walk back out on the screened-in porch and you'll see a cabinet. Think maybe it used to be full of canned goods and preserves. Cane syrup in jars. Everything painted yellow.

Now you will see a stairway. Go on up - they're fine. There used to be a double Dutch door, but Someone got it last year. My guess is that this was once the attic, then remodeled. You never saw a more comfortable-looking room! On one wall is a fireplace. French windows look out upon camillias, polka-dotted with ruby ruffles. There's a desk built into the wall, cubby-holes everywhere.

Downstairs are four rooms with a central hall. One room is almost gone - rain damage from a hole in the roof. There's a chest of drawers full of rats' nests. Of the two front rooms, I often wonder which was the living room.. Sometimes I run my hand over the wall, trying to feel vibrations.

There's a handmade railing all around the front porch. Bet there used to be some rocking chairs and maybe a porch swing! You can just barely see the road now. Sometimes the green leaves are covered with reddish dust from dry dirt.

But don't leave yet - there's more! The driveway is actually a two- rut road, leading to some marvels! First, the tool shed. Please, don't shake this building. It's apt to come down on your head! Walk carefully and note the many hooks, shelves and drawers. Screwdrivers and fish hooks turned to rust. Bet you could find anything you needed in here!

Across the road there's more cars and some farm equipment, weeds growing up through everything. Under that tin roof is where they used to work on cars and such. You can tell because of the come-along and engine parts lying around. When it's hot you can still smell grease. Bet they used to get good and dirty. Drink ice tea, not talking, just working.

Come on down the road a little bit more. The corn barn. Set up on big hunks of lighter knot. The corn husker still works - turn that wheel and you'll see! You can go in on the right side. There's a big sifter on the floor. A ladder leads up to the second story. I would of loved to see it full of corn. Bet they had some fat chickens!

There's another shed, but it's caved in pretty bad and I wouldn't recommend going in there.

One day last week, we found an old crumbly magazine, dated December, 1963. You could just barely make out the name above the mailing address. Julian C. Calhoun. Now when I come out here, I call his name in my mind -- hoping he'll answer.

Cleaning Out the Boat

Otis was cleaning out his oyster boat when Darlene walked up. "Hi, Otis!" she greeted warmly. Otis looked around and said, "Would you hand me that broom over there?" She gingerly picked the raggedy broom out of a pile of junk that looked dangerously close to collapsing.

"I clean it out once a year, whether it needs it or not," Otis declared firmly. "I believe it," sniffed Darlene.

"Would you go turn on the hose for me?" he asked. So Darlene went and turned on the hose. Bits of oyster shell and seaslime went flying as Otis turned the hose on full blast into the bow of the boat.

"Hey....watch it!" hollered Darlene as she was hit with an unidentified flying blob. "Would you go into the trailer and git me the dish soap from beside the sink?" asked Otis.

So Darlene stormed into the trailer to get the dish soap. She brought it back and handed it up to him as he continued his yearly cleaning. "Dern - you didn't bring a rag. How'm I gonna wipe this stuff up?" he complained.

So Darlene went back in the trailer and found a couple of old rags under the sink. "Hey...how about a hand up here?" he suggested. So Darlene climbed into the oyster boat and took one of the rags and began to wash the cull board down.

"I'm goin' in to git me a beer. Want one?" said Otis as he climbed out of the boat and headed into the trailer. "Yeah," she answered.

About a half hour later Darlene had gotten most of the inside of the boat washed and rinsed. "Hey, where's my beer?" she thought. So she climbed down and went inside to see what had happened to Otis. She found him lying on the couch drinking beer, watching T.V. "Hey, what in the heck are you doing? I thought you were coming in here to get me a beer," she demanded.

"I forgot. Wrestling came on and I didn't want to miss this match," he said defensively. "Well, you can take your beer and your boat and shove it!" she yelled as she slammed the door going out.

"Gee," thought Otis when she'd left, "wonder what got her all teed off?"

Black Creek Crater

During the mid-eighteen hundreds, an old woman lived on the banks of Black Creek. At times, the ferns grew so high around her house you could barely see it. She'd sit outside her tiny cabin in a straight backed rocker and watch the black water swirl past. Sweet potatoes, catfish and wild blueberries were her staple foods. The only company she got was from occasional groups of Indians following the creek southward.

New settlers in Sopchoppy heard tales of how she learned from these Indians how to speak with wild creatures. As with most tales, it grew and grew. Before long, folks were talking about how she spoke face to face with bobcats and bears. Two little boys, who were best friends, would listen, spellbound by these reports. One day they decided to sneak around there and see if she really did hold conversations with animals. They crept quietly through the woods and hid near her house.

Well, they waited and watched. Finally they saw her come out of the cabin and fling some sort of seed into the air. Pretty soon she was surrounded by wrens, redbirds and squirrels. And yes, she was talking to them!

They ran home excitedly and told everyone who would listen about what they had seen. Before long, another little boy convinced them to go back and watch the old woman talk to the creatures. Sure enough, they saw her come out and fling seeds into the air. But this time was different. This time, she caught them.

"What are you doing here?" she asked. Of course they were too scared to think up a lie, so they told her the truth. She just laughed brightly and said, "Is that so?"

"What are you going to do to us?" one of them asked.

"Send you home, of course," she replied. "And one more thing before you go.... watch the sky tonight. About an hour after sundown," she added mysteriously.

Of course, by sundown the whole town of Sopchoppy had heard about what the old woman had said. They waited in doorways, or watched through the windows. Especially three little boys.

All at once, the sky lit up with falling stars. They flew left and right and up and down. In fact, one kept getting bigger and bigger and closer and closer. Right when folks were getting really worried, it hit over by Black Creek. It burned brightly for a moment, then went out. No one dared venture over there till the next morning.

When they did, they found the old woman sitting in her rocking chair next to a huge hole in the ground. The earth and the plants had been blackened completely around the edge of the hole. She smiled sweetly at them and kept rocking as they gawked in astonishment. Finally one of the little boys asked her, "How did you know?"

She smiled that same sweet smile as before and replied. "See that little jay bird over there........?"

Author's Note: Although Black Creek has all but swallowed up the remaining part of the crater, blackened limestones still dot the area.

The Bravest Man in Pinetta

Around the turn of the century there was a man in Pinetta, Florida, who was said to be fearless. He would hunt 'gators at night without a light, and pick up rattlesnakes by the head. He was also very religious, a pious churchgoer. Some said the only thing C.C. Pickles was afraid of was the devil. One night this was proven to be true.

An ornery old man had recently passed on. He had been laid out in a house right down the road from the church. The custom in those days was to sit up all night with the dead, praying, and helping them to pass gracefully into the hands of the Lord. Afterwards, the coffin would be nailed shut to keep out varmints until it was buried. Some of the men of the church decided to see just how brave old C.C. was!

Right before dawn, when everybody was just aching to drift off to sleep, they suggested leaving C.C. there, alone with old man 'Stump' (a nickname because he only had one leg), to nail up the coffin. "Stump'll be comin'back to git his leg!" they told him. But C.C. stood his ground and said he'd be glad to. He wasn't "scarda nothin'". So they left him there with just two candles for light, a hammer and some nails. About the time they left, a hoot owl began to call and there was an unnatural chill in the air.

C.C. began to get nervous despite himself.. Well, he went to hammering. He kept missing the nails so often that by the time one side was completed, the first candle had burned out. He had almost got the other side done when the second one went. Seeing as how he had only one nail left to go, he felt around in the dark for the edge of that coffin. Then he got his nail in the right place and began pounding. But when he tried to straighten up, he couldn't! Something had got ahold of him and was pulling him back down. Well, he forgot about being brave, let out a holler, and rared back. By then, it had let go, so he tore out the door before old man "Stump" could grab him again!

By the time the funeral was held that afternoon, everyone in Pinetta had heard about old man Stump coming back for his leg.

When the pallbearers went to get his coffin, they saw what had 'grabbed' the bravest man in town.

There was a large piece of blue cloth under the last nail. C.C. had leaned over in the dark and nailed his own shirt down!

The Piano

No telling how long that piano had been sitting there. The keys were swollen and coming apart. It was an upright piano, made of dark wood which was splitting and peeling from dampness. In the front of the church, only one old pew was left. Broken glass was scattered all over the floor where windows had been broken out. Falling leaves and pine needles fluttered in the windows. Jeremy went and sat down down on the pew. He shivered...as much from cold as from the memories.

His father had been the preacher there a long time ago. He could remember coming to church in a horse-drawn buggy. Then they got the car. At first, Jeremy didn't like the idea of the car. It went so fast you couldn't see new violets in early Spring, or quail scurrying through dog fennel. Later, he became proud of it. Not many families had cars in those days.

Sunday mornings were important events. The whole family would get up early, do chores, have breakfast, and deck out in their best clothes. Every third Sunday Jeremy would get to pass the collection plate. Whereas he didn't usually think to comb his mass of red curls, he'd spend thirty minutes wetting and combing it so it would lie flat against his head. (This usually lasted only as long as it stayed wet.) It was during this period of his life that Jeremy found his calling.

A great aunt passed away and left them a piano. Jeremy soon proved to be the only one with any aptitude for using it. As the years passed, he became so good at it that he was allowed to take lessons. Jeremy's piano was eventually moved to the church and put up close to his father's podium. Folks who'd never been to church in their life would come...just to hear him play! He became popular with the young women. For the first time in his life, he was not embarrassed by his red curls and rampant freckles.

Then came the Depression of the thirties. They had to let the farm hands go and do the planting, tending and harvesting themselves. This was a time of great frustration for Jeremy, as he no longer had time to practice the piano.

His mother passed away one frozen Winter, and his father became withdrawn. He no longer took care of the farm, and quit preaching on Sundays. He died a few months later. In despair, Jeremy sold the farm and drove the car to Jacksonville. He found work in the shipyards and joined a local church. He eventually became choir director at the church, and began giving private lessons. After a while, he was able to quit the shipyard work and concentrate on his music. He had a number of private students, one of which was a very attractive young lady.

After a lengthy courtship, they got married and bought a home in Orange Park. Although they had no children, they led a contented life. He grew corn, peppers and tomatoes in the back yard. She knitted, crocheted, and took care of two cats. They grew old together. She was always rather frail, so when she came down with pneumonia, it was worse than usual. Although he sat by her bedside night and day, hoping she'd get better, she didn't. When she passed away, Jeremy was lost and frightened. He thought he'd go home to the farm.

For the first time in fifty years,. he drove those dirt roads, remembering that first car. When he reached the farmhouse, he was shocked to see a double-wide trailer sitting right where his home used to be. The big oaks out front were gone. They were replaced by two little plastic daisies that spun around whenever the wind blew.

It took some looking, but he finally found the church....abandoned for many years. As he sat there on the pew, he remembered the hymns he used to play. Shakily, he got up. It wasn't easy for an old man, but he used all his strength to move the piano back....away from the window where it wouldn't get rained on any more.

Ole Susie

Some of 'em said he was crazy --living out there in that run down farmhouse of his. It was all growed up and fallin' down. Junk was strowed all over the yard. He'd let his shock-white hair git long and his beard, too. Whenever you'd see him on the porch or in the yard he'd be carrying a rifle. Kept him some chickens out back and three or four hogs. He didn't have no dog.

My uncle said he was mean and to stay away. Which just made me want to go around there more. One day the chance came along. Everybody was gone off to some big meetin' at the church. I was playing sick, knowin' they'd go without me. They did. By the time they'd got down the road aways and you couldn't hear the truck no more, I knew it was safe. Went and got my mule, as it was too far to walk in a hurry. Just to be safe, I took my knife.

Sure enough, he was out in the yard a-sittin' on a stump. Lookin' right at me, too. I got down offen that mule and was fixin' to say "Howdy," when he said "Git!" So I began to git back on ole Susie. But Susie had other plans. She decided right then and there to set down! Well, this was highly embarrassin', as I'd been told to git. So I poked her, as this works sometimes. She didn't budge. Only thing that come to mind was to lift her backside up offen the ground sufficiently to let her know what I wanted her to do. Have you ever tried to lift a mule?

That old man was just watchin' me, his eyes narrow and mean lookin'. So I tried again. But Susie just looked around at me with them eyes a'laughin'. This was distressin' cause Susie had a mind of her own.

Well, that man just set there a'watchin me for the longest time. Directly, he got up and walked over behind the house. When he come back he was carryin' a long board. My heart like to stopped, as I thought he was fixin' to kill me right there!

"Try this," he said, handin' the board to me.

"You mean beat her with it?" I asked, knowin' that ole Susie was sure not to git up if I hit her.

"Heck no, son," he replied. "Pry her loose!"

Mozell's

In the early thirties, a feller named Al Acree bought a little chunk of land down by the Withlacoochee River. Since it was right across the line from Madison County, Fla., into Lowndes Co., Ga., he got an idea. He'd open up a liquor store. Madison Co. is dry to this very day. Folks from Madison who prefer a little spirits now and then found this highly convenient, as it was right down the road.

He ran it for a while, then acquired another place (and that's another story) A feller from around Valdosta, named Mozell Spell, bought it from Al Acree in the late thirties. Mozell loved to fish. Here was a spot where he could fish and make a little money at the same time. Little did he know that his penchant for fishing would bring him fame and fortune over the next three decades.

One day, when business was slow, Mozell caught so many catfish he decided to have a fish fry. Well, that was the beginning.

The fish fry turned out to be such a success that he had another one. And another. And another. Pretty soon he'd made enough money to build a long wooden building down by the river. He filled it with tables and benches and opened up a catfish restaurant.

This restaurant was so successful that he opened a larger restaurant right next to the liquor store. He fixed it up real nice, and hired a cook and some waitresses. His wife planted daylillies and camellias out in front. Folks could have drinks, dinner, and listen to the jukebox. For those inclined to bet a nickel once in a while, there were slot machines in back. A jovial black woman cooked the most delicious seafood you ever ate in your life. Waitresses bustled around, especially on Friday and Saturday nights. In the words of one of these veteran waitresses, weekends were "out of this world."

Although he was making lots of money, he was having to work longer hours. So he built an apartment on top of the liquor store where he could rest in between shifts. From here, he could look out at his beloved Withlacoochee, the river he didn't have time to fish in anymore.

Thirty years later, his health began to fail. He sold his business and retired to a small farm nearby. Once again, he had time to relax - and fish.

The restaurant was never reopened. The liquor store is still there, adjoining a dingy lounge with an elbow-worn wooden bar and a pool table. Vines and bushes hide what is left of the restaurant, which stands in disrepair. A weather beaten sign remains next to the highway, declaring "Mozell's" in nonexistant neon. The only thing left to suggest its former splendor is a huge camellia bush that blooms ruby red each Christmas.

One More Fishing Story

"Quit rockin' the boat," yelled Wilbur. "If you jest sit still, them fish'll never know you're there. If they think you ain't there, they'll bite them worms," he went on.

"Aw, shet up, Wilbur. You don't know nothin' 'bout fishin' noway," replied Doolan.

"Yore trouble is, you like to eat 'em, but you don't give a hoot 'bout catchin' them," Wilbur fussed. Doolan took a pinch of snuff.

"You cain't catch a fish with dip in yore mouth. It won't set right. You gotta set yore mouth right," complained Wilbur.

Doolan stuck his finger in his ear and then in his pocket. "Quit fidgetin'. You're makin' me too nervous to concentrate. Iffen you cain't concentrate, you cain't catch no fish," said Wilbur. Doolan smiled.

A little while later they both caught a fish. "See...what'd I tell you! Quit fidgetin' and set still so I can concentrate, and we caught us some fish. Don't say I didn't tell you so. That's some good lookin' fish, even if you did scare 'em away for a while," Wilbur rudely stated. Doolan opened up a Coca Cola.

Pretty soon a school of mullet started jumping all around them. "Great goodness! Set still, Doolan. They'll jump in the boat iffen you set still. Durn it - you cain't set still for nothin', can you?" hollered Wilbur. A couple of nice sized mullet jumped in the boat and began to flop around on the floor. Doolan grabbed them and stuck them in the fish bucket. "Don't jest sit there - put something on top of it," yelled Wilbur. Doolan stuck a couple of croaker sacks and a board on top of the bucket.

"That ain't goan hold. I'll jest have to do it myself. Here, put this ice chest on top of it. You ain't got no sense a'tall when it comes to fishin'," complained Wilbur as he set the ice chest on top of the bucket. Doolan grinned.

When they finally got back to the boat landing, Wilbur had to put his two cents in. "You goan knock a hole in it, Doolan," he screamed. "I gotta teach you how to fish and now I got to teach you how to land a boat. It's a dern wonder we got any fish a'tall, the way you was fidgetin' and rockin' the boat," he went on. Doolan smiled and wrapped the rope around a piling.

Wilbur's wife, Betty Lou, drove up in a truck and began to back it down to the boat trailer. "Dern it, you're fixin' to run over the trailer. To your left. To your left!" hollered Wilbur. "Why they give a woman a driver's license, I don't know. Stop! Stop!" he hollered some more.

They got the boat on the trailer and the fish in the truck. "Them'll go good with some cheese grits and hush puppies," said Betty Lou.

"Yeah, iffen you'd ever learn to cook 'em right," Wilbur put in. "You don't git the grease hot enough. You gotta git it boilin' 'fore you put the fish in. And make sure it's done. I cain't stand nothin' that ain't done," Wilbur continued.

When they got back to Wilbur's house, Doolan and Betty Lou carried the bucket onto the back porch to clean the fish. "I don't want no scales," yelled Wilbur as they walked off.

"How could you stay in that boat all day long with Wilbur?" asked Betty Lou as soon as they got around the corner. Doolan reached into his pocket and brought out a small pink object and stuck it into his ear.

"What'd you say?" he asked? "I cain't hear nothin' without my hearing aid!".

Renata's Christmas Wish

Renata was one of those divorced, middle-aged career women who give no more thought to holidays than to stick a stamp on a card or two.

"Nope, Christmas is for children!" she replied to a co-worker who asked if she had put up a tree. Every now and then she'd stare wistfully at the homes on her block whose yards were strung with lights and strewn with Christmas figurines.

On Christmas Eve she could stand it no longer. She got in her car and drove south, glad to get out of the house, and even gladder to get out of the office.

Lost in her thoughts, her car seemed to drive itself as if possessed of a will of its own. She did not realize where she was until she looked down and saw the bay beneath her. The bridge lifted her higher and higher, until she thought she'd just soar right off into the sky. It then set her gently down on St. George Island.

She checked into a room and ordered a dinner to go. She ate, showered, and dressed warmly. A walk on the beach might free her mind and loosen her tense body.

Perhaps she walked a mile. Perhaps two. An opal moon hung in the night sky and the gulf whispered in hushed dreamtones. She sat on the beach and closed her eyes, wishing for a Christmas of her very own. When she opened them, she saw that her prayers had been heard.

There on the horizon, was a small fleet of fishing boats, each one ablaze with hundreds of multi-colored lights. Their reflection sparkled and danced over the water, and landed in the sand at her feet.

Medicine Woman

Kids used to go over there all the time to see that medicine woman. She cured the bee bite and the cow-itch on those young'uns. They took a man in there one night that was snake-bit. He didn't have money for a hospital, and they didn't take such as him in those days, anyway. She cured him, but it took a solid week. When he got home, he found his brothers had skinned out the seven foot diamond- back that had bitten him. He nailed the hide onto a board and took it around to her house and set ut up by the front door.

My Grandpa Magnum told me she delivered him and all eight of his brothers and sisters. She also cured his Mama when she had those spells. She wore some kind of bone around her neck, and always smelled like camphor. Grandpa said she had taken care of most folks around here, until they got roads in and cars to drive. After that, the high-bred didn't go to her anymore. They drove down to Apalachicola to go to the regular doctor. The roads weren't too good then, and some folks died just trying to get there!

Me, I remember the time somebody's young'un got torn up by a bob cat. That child was only about three or four. Nobody thought she would live, she was bleeding so badly. There was no time to get her to the doctor, so they took her around there to that medicine woman. She stitched the little girl up so good you could hardly see the scars. Then, she had to go around with a strong-smelling bandage on for days.

Then, there was the time Uncle John got ahold of some bad moonshine. Me and one of my brothers had to go down by the river and bring her back some kind of root. She began to boil it in that old iron kettle of hers, then made us leave, as she said it was fixing to get messy in there. Uncle John quit drinking and became a preacher after that.

I just went around there the other day to get some more medicine for my rheumatism, and that derned snake hide was still on the porch. When you get to be my age, you ache. Why, next month I'll turn ninety seven. And come to think of it, that medicine woman must be getting old, too!

Kirvin's Romance

Her little white poodle had a rhinestone collar and red toenails. She wore a huge sunhat decorated with plastic flowers and birds. Her lips were as red as the little dog's toenails. She wore gold shoes and diamond rings. Every morning about ten o'clock they'd stroll down to the park, where the little white poodle would do its business and chase pigeons. She'd sit there thumbing through a movie star magazine. Kirvin thought she was the most beautiful woman he'd ever seen.

She'd walk past his house on her way to the park, and he'd make sure he was out in the yard doing something, anything, just to catch a glimpse of her. Kirvin was a widower, who tended to reclusiveness. This was the first time in twenty odd years a female had caught his eye. He just had to meet her. So he followed her to the park one day.

He sat down on the bench next to her and said, "You're new around here, aren't you?" She smiled coyly, but did not reply. So he said, "What's your little dog's name?" Again, she smiled, but gave no answer.

The next day he tried again. He sat on the bench next to her and asked, "Where did you get that lovely purple outfit?" She blushed, smiled, but made no reply. So he went to Plan B. He pulled a can of Vienna sausage out of his pocket and opened it over the grass. After pouring out the juice, he extracted a sausage and held it out for the poodle. It sniffed around cautiously, finally inching up close enough to snatch the meat and run.

The next day, she appeared in a bright pink outfit with gold stars splashed across the front. The poodle had its toenails painted to match. He sauntered up and sat down next to her. "My name's Kirvin. What's yours?" She looked at him blankly, then smiled that same dazzling smile. He gave the poodle a dog biscuit.

"What the heck are you doing chasing that woman?" asked his next door neighbor one day.

"Not much. She won't even talk to me," he answered.

"Well, just don't go making a fool of yourself," the neighbor advised.   "No fool like an old fool," Kirvin muttered sarcastically.

Embarrassed, he gave up his quest to meet the exotic stranger. Then, one day, he saw her coming down the sidewalk with Mrs. Smith, an old friend of his. Later on, he saw Mrs. Smith walking home alone. He dashed out to the sidewalk. "Hello!" he greeted.

"Kirvin! How nice to see you." replied Mrs. Smith.

"Who was that lovely woman you walked to the park with this morning?" he eagerly questioned.

"Miss Lopez - she's new in the neighborhood. Don't you just love her little dog?" she asked.

"Cute as a button," answered Kirvin.

"She's kind of hard to get to know, though," mused Mrs. Smith.

"How so?" asked Kirvin, reflecting on his own failure to do so.

"Well, for one thing, she's from Ecuador," said Mrs, Smith., and doesn't speak a word of English! "

Emanuel Dimitrios

In downtown Apalachicola, there's a law office. It sits right across from the courthouse in an area they used to call Irishtown. In the old days, this house belonged to Emanuel Dimitrios, a Greek immigrant. Emanuel had been a ship's captain, traveling so extensively that he became fluent in twelve languages. His dream was to settle in America. Luck was with him.

He happened to be on a ship docking at Ellis Island, New York. Immigration offices were there, and there was a great need for interpreters, due to the heavy flow of foreign peoples into America. He was immediately hired. America at last!

While in New York, he fell into the company of an actress. She persuaded him to come to Florida with her, but things didn't work out between them. He decided to explore Florida for a while - the balmy atmosphere reminded him of Greece. Eventually he found himself in Apalachicola, staring into the eyes of a beautiful Italian girl - Anna Martina. They were married, had children and grandchildren. She became known as 'Other Mama' to all the children of Irishtown. He became an expert net-maker and fisherman.

Through the years, Emanuel established a routine. Every evening, when the crickets began to sing on the courthouse lawn, he would go for a stroll. There are some that still remember seeing him standing next to the river, staring endlessly into its beguiling depths. He would then stop by Chauncy's or the Oasis for his evening nightcap. Around ten o'clock when the children had just been put to bed, those that were still awake could hear tap-tapping of his cane, coming closer and closer home.

A few years ago I was talking to some of his grandchildren and great nephew. They told me that long after he had died, (especially while 'Other Mama' remained in the house) they had lain there awake - listening to the tapping of his cane. In fact, there are people to this day who hear a strange tapping noise coming up a certain street in Apalachicola on warm summer evenings.

Dirt Surfing

Those boys out there in Lee have got no sense at all when it comes to dirt surfing. The first I heard of it, I thought they were either drunk or crazy. Usually, they were both. When you're stuck way out there in the country all the time, and the only thing you've got for excitement is the TV, you can think of the durndest things! Having all those dirt roads around must have given them the idea. Those fields are handy, too, when they're not full of corn.

All you need is a truck, a rope, and a board. Now, the board has to be just right. Folks that are real good usually have a custom-made board. One that's beveled off just right around the edges and has a good strong ring on it. The ring is attached to the rope, which is attached to the truck. You'd better hope you've got a good ring and a good rope. I've seen a few of them bust aloose and go spinning off into a fence or those blackberry bushes. You could be picking stickers out for a month.

In the summertime, when it's hot and dry, those dirt surfers will send up a dust cloud like you wouldn't believe. Got a wake to them like a speedboat in the river. The corn plants will be pure dusty till the next rain. The best time to dirt surf is when the sand is real dry. On those roads by the river, you can make wavy patterns for miles. Looks like a monster black snake has wriggled down the road.

Taking a curve or a turn is the hard part, so you better hope you've got a good driver. One that knows dirt surfing and has done it. You've got to slow down just right, then speed up just right to keep the surfer on the board.

Me, I'm too old and rickety to try it. The other night I dreamed I was, though. Dust clouds were spewing up on both sides, folks were watching from the sides of the road. And there I was - surfing down the road and grinning like a gol-derned fool!

Fire at the Heartbreak Hotel

It was Saturday night on West College Avenue in Tallahassee. The year, 1976. The place, the Heartbreak Hotel. Several fraternities were rocking and rolling nearby. A beautiful harvest moon shone down on the festivities.

Dee was spending a peaceful evening at home in her room at the Heartbreak Hotel. She shared the front bedroom with her boyfriend, Clay. He had turned the hurricane lantern on low, and gone to the Pastime Bar for a few beers. She fell asleep in her birthday suit, listening to the distant refrain of "Free Bird."

Two friends in the room just above hers were staying awake late that night. They were having one of their endless philosophical discussions. T.L., who lived in a converted bathroom at the end of the upstairs hallway, was fast asleep in his berth above the bathtub. Charles Gary, who lived across from them, was whittling down a water bird out of a piece of wood. The full moon shone yellow and gold through his upstairs window.

Dee awoke to the sound of crackling. Her curtains were on fire! The hurricane lantern had ignited them while she slept! Hurriedly she pulled a nearby sleeping bag around her and ran into the hall, screaming. Upstairs, the two friends looked out the window and saw flames shooting upwards. They awoke T.L., who scurried onto the roof deck with a half pound of illegal dried plant material. An Englishman, who lived across the downstairs hallway ran out of his room yelling for the 'Fire Brigade' at the top of his lungs. Charles Gary came running gallantly down the stairs with a small pan of water.

About that time, Clay came staggering in from the Pastime Bar. Being a logical person, he immediately sized up the situation. He quickly grabbed Dee's sleeping bag from around her, leaving her buck naked in the doorway, just as the Fire Department was arriving. Using it, he extinguished the flames as the firemen lingered in the hallway.

Later on, after the fire truck had left and the Heartbreak Hotel lapsed again into silence and slumber, T.L. came down from the roof. To this very day, he'll swear that the harvest moon that shone that night was wearing an unmistakable smile.

Ross Mountaion

This is how it was told to me by my father. Right outside Cataula, Ga., is a place called Mulberry Creek. There's where you'll find Ross Mountain. It's terraced all around - that being done by my (I don't know how many greats) grandfather.* He was a Ross. They grew corn and cotton in the rich mountain soil, producing abundantly year after year. ?Great grandpap built a grist mill on the creek, where they ground corn. All this was done in the early 1800s before Sherman and the Yanks came through to win back the southlands.

Life was bountiful in those days, and many children were born. Close by lived the Ham family. By the time Civil War broke out, these two families had intermarried.

Great grandpap built a store, where he sold candy, clothing, tobacco, etc. Locals also began to shop at the store. Before long he had quite a clientele!

It seems an old Indian came around one day for licorice and cigars. He paid in gold nuggets from a leather pouch around his waist. He and ?great grandpap became friends. He told wonderful stories about life in the old days, before most of his people were "relocated" to the desert. Some, like him, had hidden in caves. That's how he found the gold mine.

Some tried to follow him when he left the store, hoping he would lead them to the secret mine. They never could! He'd lose them in the woods every time! The old Indian finally died without telling anyone where it was.

Over the years, Ross Mountain eroded, perhaps covering up the entrance to the mine. Some men with shovels went up on the mountain to dig for it. They camped out that night and awakened to see the Indian's ghostly appearance floating just above the smoldering camp fire. A child wandered off into the forest and reported being led back by a kindly grey haired Indian who then vanished before his eyes.

Years later, the word was out. The Yankees were coming! A trusted uncle was chosen to carry the family valuables out to hide. The family waited in suspense, loaded up and ready to flee. The children were probably already in wagons, hitched up to the fastest horses. ?Great- uncle hurried as fast as he could, searching for a perfect hiding place.

"I've found the gold mine!" he cried as he burst in the door, sweating and puffing,. It turned out that when he went to hide the family fortune, an Indian figure appeared in the trees and led him to the gold mine, where he concealed his burden,

"Where - tell us where!" they pressed. As he struggled to regain his breath, his face turned white and he began to clutch at his chest. ?Great uncle died of a heart attack before he could tell anyone where the darn thing was!

Most of the Hams and Rosses survived the Civil War and went on to populate Georgia and Alabama. Daddy told me he had visited ?great- uncle's grist mill and that it was still standing. The mountain was still terraced and Mulberry Creek flowed on. I said,"when was this, Dad?" He thought for a minute and then replied. "Oh, I guess back in '41 or '42. Last I heard, folks were still diggin'"

[*Henceforth referred to as ?great grandpap]

The Bet

Once his mind was made up, that was it! There wasn't any use to argue, because you wouldn't be right even if you were right.

"I ain't never seen nobody as bull headed as Buck Shiver," said Wanda as she shelled acre peas over a bucket on the porch one day. "Jest oncet, I'd like to see him change his mind and admit he coulda been wrong. Jest oncet," replied Melba.

"Yeah, well, you kin wish all you want to, cause it ain't gonna happen. I been knowin' that hard-headed man since I was this tall," said Wanda. She held her hand up about three feet from the floor.

"Hit ain't no wonder his wife's gone deaf. Hit's a whole lot easier than arguin' all the time," Melba commented.

"Deaf? You shoulda seen her at the church picnic," Wanda put in. "She kin hear bettern you or me. I was a'talkin' about how her slip was always showin' down south and she was a good fifty foot aways. She come right over there and says 'what did you say about me?'"

"If that don't beat all," Melba mused.

It wasn't long after this, that they got to prove old Buck wrong and set him straight for once in his life.

Now Buck was a gambling man. Every Friday and Saturday night, he'd get together with some friends and play poker in Charlie Porter's barn. This was a ritual that had been broken only in dire emergencies over the past few years. Melba lived across the dirt road from Charlie and watched in disapproval as the men showed up around five o'clock each weekend, and headed for Charlie's barn.

Buck was always accompanied by his hound dog, Scout, who would wait patiently outside the barn door until the card game was over. Scout could tree a coon or possum in no time flat, and Buck was real proud of him. All he had to do was say "Git 'em, Scout!" and that critter was as good as treed.

One Saturday, Melba heard a whump out back of her house. She ran around there and found that a large coon had fallen into her trash can and couldn't get out. She went inside and called Wanda to come over. "Hope Buck's in a bettin' mood and has plenty of cash!" laughed Melba as they formulated their plan.

About an hour later, the men were interrupted by Melba's cries from across the road. They reluctantly put down their cards and peered out of the barn to see what was going on. A large coon was on Melba's front porch eating her freshly shelled butterbeans. Buck grinned as he pulled out his wallet. "How long do you think it will take Scout to tree that coon?" he asked. As they got out a pocket watch and took bets on the time, Wanda and Melba watched them from the window and tried not to bust out laughing.

"Git 'em, Scout!" hollered Buck, knowing he was going to win on his minute and a half bet. Scout dashed off, his nose to the ground, picking up the scent of that coon. Like a flash, he ran across the road. Buck began to jump up and down in his excitement. Then -- all of a sudden, Scout stopped, looked around, and began sneezing. He looked up the road, down the road, then finally ran back to his master, snorting and snuffling. Buck watched Scout in disbelief as the coon eyed them suspiciously, then went back to eating butterbeans.

Meanwhile, back at Melba's house, the two women laughed until they couldn't laugh any more. "Did you see his face when Scout started sneezing?" giggled Melba. "Hit was worth ever one'a them butterbeans!" she added.

"You couldn't a'cooked 'em, anyway - you're all out of pepper!" howled Wanda as she held up the empty shaker.

Nightmare Remedy

There was not a thing in the world he hated more than a barking dog in the middle of the night. It startled him awake, and he could not finish his dream no matter how hard he tried. That same noise was welcome when he was having a nightmare, but lately his dreams had been good. He attributed this to the concoction Rena had given him. She lived down by the creek with her two sons and about forty cats. She'd given him the nightmare remedy because he'd complained so badly about his unpleasant dreams.

"There's no need for that," she'd announced. "I'll fix you up a little brew of mine." Rena was famous for her "little brew." Country folks came all the way from neighboring counties for her potion. Them that hadn't slept good in years were heard saying what a good night's sleep they'd had. Lemuel just recently found out that this potion would also improve the quality of his dreams.

He'd been tormented by nightmares ever since he was five years old and found what was left of Aunt Lucy in the hog pen. The pastor said he'd grow out of it. And he did, partially. Though the nightmare didn't seem to come so often anymore, it seemed to grow more intense. The hogs were rushing at him as someone called "Su-ee!" in the background. He would trip and fall, looking backwards at the hogs.... teeth bared and hungry.....coming for him. He'd wake up then, hot and sweaty and terrified. Rena's nightmare remedy had worked so far, and it had been two months since he'd had one.

When the mayonnaise jar full of potion ran low, he'd hightail it over to Rena's to get some more. Most of the time she'd be in the kitchen. There was a big garden full of fresh greens and tomatoes outside her kitchen door. Her two boys were tall and gangly and quiet. They kept the wood chopped and the yard clean. But the kitchen was Rena's domain. No one was ever allowed in there and she kept the kitchen door locked, except when she went out to feed her cats. There was always a strange smell coming from inside that kitchen and several times Lemuel tried to peek around the kitchen door. Rena would always scold him for this, so he quit. After all, she had her secrets.

A few days later, Lemuel saw the ambulance go by. Mrs. Smith from next door came up on the porch where he was sitting and told him it was Rena. Later on, he found out that she'd had a stroke and never recovered.. Her funeral came and went. The mayonnaise jar was almost empty and he wondered what he was going to do. Those hogs were sure to chew him up tonight or the next, or the next. It was either stay awake or go see Rena's boys.

He found them out back picking collards. The oldest he judged to be about eighteen and the younger one wasn't much behind that. Their solemn eyes and respectful ways made him feel more at ease, so he asked them if Rena'd had anymore nightmare remedy made up.

"Why, sure, Lemuel. We got plenty. Come on in and we'll fetch you some," the oldest replied. Whatever the secret of the kitchen was, the boys knew about it. To his surprise, they led him right into that kitchen! It was filled with shelves from the floor to the ceiling. Those shelves were filled with bottles and bottles of something. They took his jar and filled it from one of the bottles. "Here ya go," they said. "Some of Mama's homemade fox-grape wine!"

Miracle On St. George

On St. George Island, you have to live with the threat of violent storms, tornados, tidal waves and hurricanes. There's one story that's been going around this area since the early nineteen hundreds. It's a tale of survival - a man and his horse!

Back in those days, settlers were sparse. This was mainly due to the heat, bugs, snakes, and lack of a bridge to get there. This one old settler was tough as bear gristle and twice as determined. He had made up his mind to live out his days in an "island paradise." He owned a horse that was just as tough and determined. It is said the horse preferred sandspurs to hay! The old man lived on seafood and a few supplies from town, which he rowed across the bay once or twice a month. No one ever saw him buy spirits, but he always was said to have a bottle of rum handy. Some think he found a shipwreck, close to where the Cut (a man-made waterway) is now. One that was bound for Apalachicola from the West Indies with a hold full of rum!

One year there was a terrible hurricane, which brought with it a nine foot tidal wave from the bay side. That night the old man and his horse went out floundering, trying to ignore almost impossible winds. Suddenly there was a flash of lightning, illuminating the whole bay. In that instant, they saw it coming! He dropped those fish and climbed a tall pine tree as fast as he could, then looked back at his horse and yelled, "Hold on! It's a'comin'" That tidal wave loomed closer and closer, blacker and blacker with every flash of lightning.

When it finally subsided, the old man had a supply of fresh flounder to last a month! All he had to do was walk around and pick them up. And in case you're wondering how the horse survived, they say he just braced up, dug in, and held his breath!

A Family Thanksgiving

"Mildred, would you please wash the glasses first? You know the rule – glasses, then silverware, then plates, then pots and pans." commanded her Aunt Lucille. "Well, I know you were President of the Homemakers Club, Class of 32, but someone's invented this marvelous machine, called a dishwasher." replied Mildred dourly. "No need to get uppity." snarled her Aunt Lucille.

"Oooo! Lookit that short skirt!" squealed Mildred's teenage daughter, Tootie. "Well, I'll be derned, she's shown up for Thanksgiving half naked." muttered Aunt Lucille as she took her place in the living room. Cousin Marlene sauntered up the front steps in her short black skirt, just grinning away.

"Where'd you get that outfit, darlin'? Out of the back of the closet? 'Cause it looks like the rats ate the bottom half of your skirt." remarked Mildred as she stood in the doorway. "What – this?" cooed Marlene sweetly as she rolled her eyes. "Well, thank goodness the men are all out back, shucking oysters." said Aunt Lucille loud enough for everyone to hear her. Marlene pretended not to notice.

Mildred finally got out of the way long enough for Marlene to make her way into the living room, where she promptly sat down by her Aunt Lucille, who was doing a slow burn at the sight of that short skirt. Well, Marlene just went on like it was the most natural thing in the world, and everyone calmed down in a little bit.

Mildred and her sister, Shasta, were just taking the turkey out of the oven, when a loud bang went off in the back yard. Aunt Lucille clapped her hand over her heart and sucked in air. Mildred and Shasta immediately dropped the hot pan of turkey, which went skidding off across the kitchen floor. "Would yu'all just settle down? They're shootin' off the gun, as usual." explained Tootie in her most condescending voice.

"Sounds like a goldarned cannon to me." said Aunt Lucille under her breath as she heaved herself back into the easy chair. "Gun?" asked Marlene, "I just love guns!" "On Lord." moaned

Mildred as Marlene took off out the back door to see the gun. About that time, the baby woke up.

"Would someone please go get that baby!" hollered Aunt Lucille as soon as the baby let out one squeak. "Don't have a fit, I'm comin'" said Mildred in exasperation. "if you let 'em howl, it damages their lungs." scolded Aunt Lucille "Yeah, right." murmured Mildred as she scurried into the baby's room.

"Somebody check the oven – there's smoke pouring out!" yelled Aunt Lucille. But no one heard her, or felt like responding. Suddenly Shasta ran into the kitchen, pulled out the pan of burning rolls, and let out a stream of cuss words like you wouldn't believe. "Put a cork in it, Shasta!" yelled Aunt Lucille.

"What's burning?" hollered Jake (Mildred's husband) from the back yard. "You can't smell a dadblame thing unless it's burning, can you?" shouted Mildred from the baby's room. "Don't get your dern britches in a wad." said Shasta as she dumped the blackened rolls into the garbage can. "Well, it's true..." started Mildred before turning her attention to the baby, who was now swelling up in hives.

"That child is deformed. Why didn't anyone tell me? said Aunt Lucille when she saw the baby in full allergic reaction. "Tootie! Did you let the baby eat strawberries again?" asked Mildred impatiently. "He ate only three." scowled Tootie. Don't just stand there – get me the benedryl." Admonished Mildred as she rocked the baby back and forth.

"I'll just wash this here turkey off and no one will know the difference." muttered Shasta as she speared the hot turkey with two large cooking forks. Just as she heaved it into the sink, she realized that she had plopped it down into the side that held the soapy water.

Meanwhile, Marlene was out back, mesmerizing the menfolk and fixing to shoot off a .357 Magnum. "Now you hold it like this, with both hands." said Bob (Shasta's husband) patronizingly as he put his arms around her and held her hands in the right position. "Lemme show her how." said Jake. Just as she aimed at the beer can on the fence post and started to pull the trigger, Shasta leaned out the back door and hollered, "Would you get your fool hands off Marlene?"

Bob jerked back suddenly, which caused Marlene to squeeze the trigger and shut her eyes at the same time. "You just blew out two windows in Aunt Lucille's new cadillac!" screamed Shasta. Everyone came running to see the damage, except Aunt Lucille, who was unable to get out of her chair, because she had fainted.

"Oh my God! Aunt Lucille had a heart attack and died!" yelled Tootie from the living room. So everyone rushed in there. After it was ascertained that she had only fainted and not died, Shasta remembered that she'd left the turkey soaking in hot soapy water in the kitchen sink. "Uh oh." She thought as she slipped back into the kitchen.

Well, Mildred finally got the baby back to sleep and the hives were starting to disappear. Shasta had managed to wrestle the turkey into the other side of the sink and rinse it off thoroughly (she thought). She was still seeing Bob with his arms around Marlene as she attempted the classic shooter's pose. She'd just deal with him (and her) later.

Aunt Lucille had put down three glasses of sherry and was starting to see double. Tootie and Marlene were in Tootie's room discussing makeup and hair styles while the men were out back discussing Marlene. Jake brought out the Jim Beam and the men proceeded to drain the whole half-gallon.

Eventually, everyone made their way into the dining room for the Thanksgiving meal. Shasta had ole Bob propped up with one elbow, because he kept sliding off the chair. Soap bubbles continued to trickle down the side of the turkey, and the baby had awakened once more, screaming at the top of his lungs. Mildred now had him on her lap, attempting to restrain him from lunging repeatedly at the strawberry shortcake.

And, as usual, Aunt Lucille, insisted on saying the blessing. "Thank you, dear Lord, for bringing our family together once more on Thanksgiving, in peace, love, and perfect harmony." She said as she reached for the bottle of sherry.

Goose Pasture

They'd been picnicking and fishing at Goose Pasture all day. The little children were asleep in the car, their mothers nearby, picking up paper plates and plastic forks. The men were inspecting some artifacts they'd dove up that afternoon. Tools, arrowheads and pottery shards were laid out on a picnic table. Daniel had just opened a bottle of Wild Turkey when they heard the scream.

It echoed off the water and rolled around in the pine trees for a while, then stopped. Everyone froze, listening fearfully. One of the men went to his truck and got out his gun. "Guess we'd better go see about it," they agreed.

The two women gathered up the rest of the cooking stuff and got into the car. "We're taking the kids home. Y'all go see about it," they told the men. So Bob and Daniel rode off into the swampy pine forest to find out who had screamed. When they got down the road aways, they heard another scream.

"Reckon we ought to git the sheriff?" Daniel asked. "That'll take too long. Somebody might be snake bit." replied Bob. They both took a swallow of the fiery liquid and kept on, even though it was beginning to get dark. Every time they thought about giving up and going back to Perry, they heard another scream.

It wasn't long before they realized there were two screams, one lower pitched than the other. "Maybe it's banshees!" Bob said. "You'd better lay off that Wild Turkey!" replied Daniel. Pretty soon they came to the river again. The two screams seemed to be getting closer and closer together. "I can hear it right over thisaway," whispered Bob.

As they approached the river, Bob cut the headlights and turned off the truck. They sat there in silence for awhile as the moon rose over the pine trees,. full and silvery. They waited.

Another scream pierced the night. This time it was the higher pitched scream and it was right by the truck. Bob and Daniel hunkered down in the seat, glancing anxiously out the windows, hoping to see what it was. When they did, they both burst out laughing. The empty Wild Turkey bottle landed with a thump in the sand as they drove away.

Later on, when it was quiet again, the black panther resumed his love song. It echoed off the banks of the river and disappeared into the warm night air.

Shooting the Moon

Back in the eighties, a British film company came to St. George Island to make a movie. Of course, the locals were all excited at these goings-on. Business was booming, and folks had something to talk about besides each other.

Now a job as an extra in the up-coming movie paid real good. Plus, the food was excellent. Long tables were set out daily, heaped with tasty cuisine by the film company's cooking staff. Famous faces were everywhere.Then a scene was to be shot in the boat basin. It was a tranquil scene - oystermen tonging away at invisible oysters, while wives or friends manned the cull boards. A group of islanders who owned oyster boats were hired to play this part.

They all arrived promptly at 10 A.M., eagerly perching themselves on the oyster boats. By noon the film crew had still not arrived, and a sumptuous lunch was served. By two o'clock, everyone had talked themselves out and were getting bored and restless. So they went to a nearby bar and had a little something to liven up the wait. It worked.

By four o'clock folks were diving off the boats, starting water fights, and generally having a ball. After several more trips to the bar, they forgot all about being in a movie.

Of course, someone had to moon someone else. This led to a lively mooning session, with two individuals being named King and Queen of the moon. It was about this time that someone noticed the film crew gathered around - smiling and waving as the cameras rolled!

Egg Fight

Easter Sunday came around in a blaze of brilliant sunlight Azalea bushes were in full bloom and white spireas hung in graceful curves. Everyone had gone off to church, leaving Granmaw Ellie asleep in her rocking chair. Two watchful cats lay at her feet. The curtains shifted on a warm Spring breeze.

Granmaw Ellie dreamed of an Easter morning long ago. Women wore long skirts and did their hair in elaborate fashions. Men wore derbys and moustaches. Her family drove to town in a buggy to attend church for Easter services. She loved seeing the ladies' Easter hats - decorated lavishly with flowers, feathers, and painted fruit. There would be an Easter egg hunt in the churchyard later, then another when they got back home. All the kinfolk would be there and she looked forward to playing with her cousins. The dinner table would be piled high with ham, fried chicken, field peas and sweet potato pie. There would be cornbread, biscuits, and cane syrup. Children had their own table set apart from the adults, except for the babies, who had to be fed.

It was the style to plait ribbons into your hairdo and Ellie's sister had woven a bright pink one into Ellie's dark hair. She could see a blue Easter egg peeking out from behind a bush in the churchyard. It would be the first one found, she thought. Perhaps some of the boys would start an egg fight. Ellie could throw as good as any of them. She hoped they would.

They did. Ellie even got to throw a few before the grown-ups stopped them. Got one boy right up side the head. She smiled in her sleep.

"Granmaw?" someone said. She opened her eyes and found herself back in the rocking chair with the two cats curled up at her feet. "Come and watch the kids hunt Easter eggs," urged her son Arnold. Arnold had three wide-open, unruly boys. "I'd love to," she replied.

They went out onto the porch where they could see the children running wildly around, gathering the eggs for their

Easter baskets. Her daughter handed her a small wicker basket of painted, hard- boiled eggs and candies.

She selected a not-quite-done boiled egg that was painted fire-engine red. "Perfect," she thought as she lifted it from the basket, her eyes sparkling mischievously.

Fuller

West Tennessee Street was his home. During the day, he'd wander the sidewalks talking to himself. His brown curls would bounce every time he'd nod his head in agreement with himself. Some folks thought he was a burned out bum. Others considered him to be a saint or sage. At night, he'd seek out the dark shelter of the Pastime Bar. Someone would always buy him a beer and try to make sense of his conversations (which were mainly with himself.)

Miss Kitty, the wizened bartender, always kept an eye on him. She'd more than likely find him hidden under a table or bench in the morning, fast asleep. Fuller knew how to get by.

He had a check that came in every month from somewhere. The waitresses at Jerry's Restaurant knew that around the first of the month they'd be seeing a lot of Fuller. He'd slink through the front door, cowering and smiling and whispering something to himself. Those folks who knew Fuller would surround him protectively as the scowling waitresses circled.

One of Fuller's regular havens was an old house on College Avenue, called the Heartbreak Hotel. This grand relic housed artists and students in various rooms on either side of the 'dog-trot' hallway. The doors were always open. At the back of the house was a kitchen and bathroom. This was where Fuller took his showers, fully clothed. You could always tell when he'd been there because of the muddy footprints leading from the bathtub out the back door.

One day a beekeeper stopped at the Heartbreak Hotel to visit. He had a bunch of beehives in the back of his truck. Now, he halfway believed that Fuller was some sort of mystic. After he'd been there awhile, he stood up to leave. When he reached the front door, there was Fuller, running full speed with all of the bees behind him.

Now everyone took this as a sign that Fuller was indeed some sort of magical fellow. The next morning, however, those waitresses at Jerry's refused to bring him extra syrup for his pancakes. It seems he'd spilled an entire bottle onto his beard and down his shirt the day before!

Author's footnote: Fuller escaped this incident completely unharmed. Perhaps he possessed a little bit of magic after all!

John Frank

Now John Frank made a little 'shine as did lots of folks in those days. He was short, skinny, and ornery as the dickens. This must have been because he had one leg that was longer than the other. Although he was not a big man, he didn't put up with much. This was because of that dead serious look he got in his eyes when he got aggravated. Some say he once stared a bobcat down!

He maintained a still out in the Hickstown swamp, between Madison and Greenville. There was some fine 'shine that came out of that still, some say. You could light it and it would burn with a blue flame. Well, that 'shine got a little too famous. The revenoors heard about it.

They sneaked around there about the same time old John Frank was sitting there having a drink with a couple of friends. John Frank had ears as good as a bulldog's and heard those revenoors coming through the bushes long before they got there. John Frank and his friends began to high-tail it. The revenoors chased them for a while. Then, the afternoon sun got real hot and those revenoors got real tired. They'd given up on the other two and were concentrating on John Frank.

Finally, one of them caught sight of his hat. Because of his legs not being the same length, that hat was bobbing up and down. The revenoor stopped, looked back at the still full of good moonshine, and hollered, "Let's call it off, boys. We'll never catch him! He's riding a mule!"

Sally Strikes Gold

Johnny and me had been married forever. We'd raised four children and had just recently moved into his mother's 1800s plantation style house. She'd passed away shortly after we moved in, leaving us with the cleaning job of the century. Johnny, of course, thought his part of the job included mowing the grass and carrying out the garbage, period! It was about that time that Sally bought the other old plantation house down the road. Actually, I was glad she had bought it, because it was an eyesore. Then I got to know Sally ... Miss Hollywood, U.S.A.

She had platinum blonde hair that couldn't possibly be her natural color by any stretch of the imagination. Her fabulously wealthy fifth husband had just conveniently had a heart attack and left her a fortune to play with. That's when she decided to buy her very own southern plantation home and remodel it for all the magazines to photograph.

She spent a whole week taking out the pukey green carpet that had been installed sometime during the fifties. Then another week, ripping down that cheap paneling that's supposed to look like real wood but doesn't.I could just imagine her sitting on a leopard-skin covered couch in her black dressing gown with a martini in her hand. Sally was like that - very dramatic. She'd had some minor success on Broadway years (I mean YEARS) ago and it had affected her mind ever since.

Then she invited Johnny and me over to look at paint samples with her. How interesting. At least I knew she had sense enough to pick up a twelve-pack before inviting Johnny anywhere. When we arrived she brought out the Budweiser and some pretzels that were hard enough to crack your teeth unless you had falsies. We sat around a low table in the middle of the enormous living room and she brought out a book of paint samples. Those little colored squares you can hold up next to your other stuff to see how it looks. Johnny wasn't interest in anything but the free beer, so he was no help. It all started when I began tapping on the walls to find the crossbeams.

Now Sally doesn't know how to do anything practical. Mostly, all she does is try to look like Jayne Mansfield. Cigarette holders and slinky dresses. That was her! I was getting irritated, since I was the only one taking an active part in the serious stuff. I banged on the wall so hard, it caved in. That's how we found the secret passageway.

Johnny finally hoisted his dead weight off the chair and came over to help me rip out the damaged section of the wall. "Darn thing was rotten,anyway," he commented so we wouldn't have to pay for my accident.

"Do you know how old this house is?" I asked

"The foundation is brick. That would make it mid-eighteen hundreds, I suppose," Sally answered in her know-it-all manner.

We went inside the passageway after Johnny roused himself enough to go get a flashlight. The passageway led to a thick wooden door with a brass knob. Cautiously, we opened the door and shone the flashlight inside. A stairway led down.

"Who's going first?" asked Sally, to indicate it wouldn't be her.

"Is there a man in the house?" I commently subtly, for once glad I was the other gender.

"Who, me?" answered Johnny as he popped another beer.

We descended the stairway in typical scared-to-death progress. "There's bound to be spiders and snakes. Go a little slower," suggested Sally.

"They usually wait for the last one," I said wickedly. She started to light one of those skinny cigarettes with the little designs on it.

"Don't light that!" Johnny said. "There's some kind of underground gas that'll explode. I read it in Reader's Digest."

"That's right," I added, having read the same article, as it had been in our bathroom for a year and a half.

When we got to the bottom of the stairway, there was a tunnel. It had cobwebs growing all in it and smelled kind of funny. At this point, we came to our senses and decided to explore later, after we'd had more beer and run an extension cord down for better light. But when we reached the top, the door had shut and Johnny couldn't bust it open. "Oh, s____!" we all said at once.

"Well, we can't stay here. We've got to get out," I heard myself say. So we climbed back down and entered the tunnel. We inched along, actually holding hands at some point. Well, we made it through the bats and we made it through the bugs, and we made it past a huge rat that looked definitely rabid! When we reached the end of the tunnel, Johnny stumbled over something. Probably rocks, I thought. But it wasn't rocks. It was gold coins.

At least Sally was decent enough to split what we'd found. She got on the local news and is now a celebrity around here. And she's gone and decorated up that old place like a lunatic deco artist with insomnia. I've added a sensible screened-in back porch, and my Johnny's taken up fishing as a hobby, which at least gives the TV a break.

The Legend of Marty Mackin

Marty Mackin was always said to possess superhuman strength. He was large and muscular, with red hair and the bluest eyes you ever saw. He had a certain aura of invincibility and confidence. Tattoos were obscured by the thick hair on each arm. Back in those days, you couldn't be around him for long without laughing! He was full of fun and daring.

That's how I remembered him the summer of '91, when I was back in his hometown. One night I was down in a local tavern and ran into some of his old 'running buddies.' You never knew what Marty was gonna do next, they told me. Why, one night out Mosely Hall way, someone dared him to let a car drive over his chest. He did so, then got up and lifted the car right up in the air! "I seen him do it!" they both declared.

Called his sister, Myrtle, the next day, and found out they were living in a house out close to the Interstate. Pulled up in the yard shortly after, anxious to get all the details of this famous episode. Myrtle was cleaning corn. Pulling off the husks, cutting out the worm holes, and brushing them good to get the silk off.

"Wha'd you hear now?" she asked.

"Heard that Marty laid down in the road and let a car drive over him! Is it true?"

"Naw," she replied. "That ain't true." My excitement fell a little. Wouldn't hurt to ask Marty anyway.

"Where's he at?" I asked.

"In there," she said, pointing to the living room. "He don't feel good today."

Marty was watching T.V. Next to him, on a table, was a pile of pill bottles and such. His red hair had thinned and turned gray. Those brilliant blue eyes were dimmed behind thick bifocals. He puffed listlessly on a Winston. "Marty," I chirped, hating to disturb him. "Just heard that you let a car drive over you, then picked it up! Is it true?

"Naw, it ain't true," he replied. My spirits sank a little more. Hoped maybe he'd tell me <u>another</u> story anyway.

"It was a truck!" he laughed.

Dumb Dern Dogs

It wasn't anything but hot. No wind. No clouds. Just the hottest dad-blame summer I can remember. We were just kind of lolly- gagging around...that's all you can do when it gets that hot. Around about that time, the dogs started barking.

Now, I knew that when it was that hot, the dogs didn't bark nor get out from under the truck unless it was an emergency. So I got up and walked over to the window. Didn't see a thing. Those dogs were barking at nothing! Dumb dern dogs, I thought.

Then I took a nap. When I woke up, those dogs were at it again. So I walked outside to have a look. Walked around the truck where those dogs were going crazy. Didn't see anything. Dumb dern dogs, I thought again.

Later on, I felt like running down to the Suwannee Swifty for some Honey Bee and a Coca Cola. When I got close to the truck, the dogs went to barking again. Ran around that truck just howling and carrying on. Looked all around the yard and over by the shed. Didn't see a thing. Those dogs have been in the heat too long, I thought.

Well, I started to get in the truck, when Booger, my hound dog, jumped up on me. He hit me square in the chest and knocked me down. That's when I saw the rattler.

It came out of that truck striking so hard I would have been bitten for sure, if it wasn't for Booger. Then those dogs ran it off while I was standing there wondering when my heart attack was going to happen.

Well, it didn't. I calmed down and quit shaking about an hour later. I have a habit of leaving my truck door open. Figure that rattler must have crawled up in there. Maybe it was trying to get out of the heat. Field mice get in the truck sometimes. Maybe it was after one of them. I'll never know. One thing I do know. I'll never call those dern dogs dumb again!

Cream Pie

"Ain't no need to get excited," said Louis.

"You say. A woman's a woman, but a jealous woman's a dangerous animal," Cleaster stated nervously.

"How come you had to go messin' around with Ruth Ann when you had a perfectly good cook to begin with?" asked Everly.

"Cookin' ain't everything," grinned Cleaster.

"Bet me. I kin steady eat fer half an hour three or four times a day. That lasts a dern sight longer than playin' hoochie coochie," Louis put in, rubbing his huge belly.

"Thing is, I ain't sure she seen me with Ruth Ann. Iffen I knew for sure, I could figure out what to do," Cleaster speculated.

"Meanin' stay or leave town," Everly put in ominously.

"Only one way to find out," Louis mused.

"You should be able to tell right away," whispered Cleaster.

"You jest stay put and lay low," warned Louis. Cleaster was hidden under some croaker sacks on the floorboard of the back seat. Everly and Louis sat up front, headed for Emmy's house to find out if she was mad or not. When they got there, Everly and Louis went up and knocked on the door. They knew before she opened it that she was cooking something good. The smell of pie wafted out and drifted into the yard, making Cleaster's mouth water as he lay scrunched up on the backseat floorboard.

Emmy answered the door with an apron on and streaks of flour across one cheek.

"Is Cleaster here?" asked Everly.

"Nope. I'm cooking a surprise for when he does get here, though," she answered.

"Smells mighty fine," commented Louis hopefully. Emmy smiled and led them into the kitchen. A pot was simmering on the stove, and several cream pies sat on the counter cooling. "Is that coconut cream?" hinted Louis.

"Help yourself," invited Emmy.

"Dern it, what took y'all so long?" asked Cleaster, sitting up for the first time in an hour and a half.

"Pie!" said Everly and Louis in unison. "Best coconut cream I eat since Aunt Virginia died, and she was the Pie Queen." Louis went on. "Yeah...and she said they was to surprise you!" Everly added.

"Coconut cream? My favorite! Emmy ain't mad after all!" Cleaster yelled happily. "Turn this car around. I'm goin' to get my surprise!"

They pulled up at Emmy's house and Cleaster got out, grinning like a Cheshire cat. He combed his hair, straightened his collar, and knocked on the door. As she opened it, he gave her his most charming look. "Emmy, darlin'..." he started as the first pie hit him.

Why Yankees Move Down South

Some folks think yankees move down south for the weather. It ain't so! Let me tell you how I know. Ole Joe Odom passed away and his kids decided to sell his place. They chopped it up into lots, which they sold for a right good price. Willy bought the lot right next to me. He was a bald-headed skin-flinted man from up north.

First thing I noticed was where he built his house. He put it right close to the road where he didn't have no front yard. I went over there to point this out, and he said he didn't want to have to mow the lawn anymore. I said, "Willy, if you hadn't cut down all your good shade trees, you wouldn't a had to." But did he listen? You guessed it. Instead, he put a little conrcrete strip across the front where he could park his car.

Then I says, "Willy, where's your winders? I ain't never seen nobody build a house with no winders."

"This way the air-conditioning stays in and the burglars stay out," he says. This was one way I learned yankees don't move here for the weather. They keep the air-conditioner turned up so high it always feels like Detroit, Michigan.

Then, when they was finishing up his house, I went over there and says, "Willy, where's your porch? Where you gonna sit in the evenings? " But did I get a sensible answer? You guessed it.

"I'll be sitting in front of the T.V. like I always do," he told me. Those yankees would rather listen to the weather man than look at the sky to see what's coming.

Not long after Willy moved in, we had us a good hurricane. Willy come over and says, "Boarding up your windows? That's one job I don't have to do." Well, instead of making a smart reply, I just kept on hammering. We'd see who had the last laugh.

When that hurricane hit, it rained for four days. The little concrete strip Willy had for a front yard filled slam up like a swimming pool. I says, "Willy, you better move your car over to my yard where it won't get ruint." So he moved it over here.

Then, the lights went out. Willy couldn't see nothin' because he didn't have no winders. So I says, "Willy, come on over to my house where you can see."

That hurricane did its durndest, then finally blew over. Course, it took several weeks to get electricity and we had to use bottled water. That's when Willy took to sittin' on the front porch with me in the evenings. His house was like an oven, cause it couldn't get no air.

Two months later, Willy was still at my house. I says, "Willy, why don't you sell that house that ain't got no yard and no porch and no winders? You can move in the extra bedroom." So he moved in here and sold his house to the only kind of folks that would buy a house like that - more yankees. That's when I figured out why they move down here in the first place -- - to get some sense!

About the Author

Betsy James has always been fascinated by the art of storytelling. Her uncle, Billy Fielder (deceased), a well-known columnist and editor from South Carolina, was always spinning yarns when she was a child.

In an attempt to preserve the unique culture of her native North Florida, she's spent many years recording the stories told in her series of books, *Sandspurs and Sawgrass – a collection of stories from North Florida.*

She graduated from the University of South Florida with a bachelor's degree in Advanced Liberal Arts. She also spent five years at Florida Agricultural and Mechanical University, studying flute and dance.

She now resides in Madison, Florida, with her teenage son and elderly father.

Printed in the United States
53122LVS00002B/259-285

9 781587 210419